Despatch Rider

Ariel

Despatch Rider

The Experiences of a British Army Motorcycle Despatch Rider During the Opening Battles of the Great War in Europe

W. H. L. Watson

LEONAUR

Despatch Rider: the Experiences of a British Army Motorcycle Despatch Rider During the Opening Battles of the Great War in Europe
by W. H. L. Watson

Published by Leonaur Ltd

ISBN: 978-1-84677-384-6 (hardcover)
ISBN: 978-1-84677-383-9 (softcover)

http://www.leonaur.com

Publisher's Note

The opinions expressed in this book are those of the author and are not necessarily those of the publisher.

Contents

Introduction: A Letter. . . .

To 2nd Lieut. R.B. Whyte
1st Black Watch
B.E.F.

My Dear Robert—

Do you remember how in the old days we used to talk about my first book? Of course it was to be an Oxford novel full of clever little character-sketches—witty but not unkind: of subtle and pleasurable hints at our own adventures, for no one had enjoyed Balliol and the city of Oxford so hugely: of catch-words that repeated would bring back the thrills and the laughter—*Psych. Anal.* and *Steady, Steady!* of names crammed with delectable memories—the Paviers', Cloda's Lane, and the notorious Square and famous Wynd: of acid phrases, beautifully put, that would show up once and for all those dear abuses and shams that go to make Oxford. It was to surpass all Oxford Novels and bring us all eternal fame.

You remember, too, the room? It was stuffy and dingy and the pictures were of doubtful taste, but there were things to drink and smoke. The imperturbable Ikla would be sitting in his chair pulling at one of his impossibly luxurious pipes. You would be snorting in another—and I would be holding forth ... but I am starting an Oxford novelette already and there is no need. For two slightly senior contemporaries of ours have already achieved fame. The hydrangeas have blossomed. "The Home" has been destroyed by a Balliol tongue. The flower-girl has died her death. The Balliol novels have been written—and my first book is this.

We have not even had time to talk it over properly. I saw you on my week's leave in December, but then I had not thought of making a book. Finally, after three months in the trenches you came home in August. I was in Ireland and you in Scotland, so we met at Warrington just after midnight and proceeded to staggering adventures. Shall we ever forget that six hours' talk, the mad ride and madder breakfast with old Peter M'Ginn, the solitary hotel at Manchester and the rare dash to London? But I didn't tell you much about my book.

It is made up principally of letters to my mother and to you. My mother showed these letters to Mr Townsend Warner, my old tutor at Harrow, and he, who was always my godfather in letters, passed them on until they have appeared in the pages of 'Maga.' I have filled in the gaps these letters leave with narrative, worked the whole into some sort of connected account, and added maps and an index.

This book is not a history, a military treatise, an essay, or a scrap of autobiography. It has no more accuracy or literary merit than letters usually possess. So I hope you will not judge it too harshly. My only object is to try and show as truthfully as I can the part played in this monstrous war by a despatch rider during the months from August 1914 to February 1915. If that object is gained I am content.

Because it is composed of letters, this book has many faults.

Firstly, I have written a great deal about myself. That is inevitable in letters. My mother wanted to hear about me and not about those whom she had never met. So do not think my adventures are unique. I assure you that if any of the other despatch riders were to publish their letters you would find mine by comparison mild indeed. If George now could be persuaded...!

Secondly, I have dwelt at length upon little personal matters. It may not interest you to know when I had a pork-chop—though, as you now realise, on active service a pork-chop is extremely important—but it interested my mother. She liked to know whether I was having good and sufficient food, and warm things on my chest and feet, because, after all, there was a time when I wanted nothing else.

Thirdly, all letters are censored. This book contains nothing but the truth, but not the whole truth. When I described things that were actually happening round me, I had to be exceedingly careful—and when, as in the first two or three chapters, my letters were written several weeks after the events, something was sure to crop up in the meantime that unconsciously but definitely altered the memory of experiences....

We have known together two of the people I have mentioned in this book—Alec and Gibson. They have both advanced so far that we have lost touch with them. I had thought that it would be a great joy to publish a first book, but this book is ugly with sorrow. I shall never be able to write "Alec and I" again—and he was the sweetest and kindest of my friends, a friend of all the world. Never did he meet a man or woman that did not love him. The Germans have killed Alec. Perhaps among the multitudinous Germans killed there are one or two German Alecs. Yet I am still meeting people who think that war is a fine bracing thing for the nation, a sort of national week-end at Brighton.

Then there was Gibson, who proved for all time that nobody made a better soldier than the young don—and those whose names do not come into this book....

Robert, you and I know what to think of this Brighton theory. We are only just down from Oxford, and perhaps things strike us a little more passionately than they should.

You have seen the agony of war. You have seen those miserable people that wander about behind the line like pariah dogs in the streets. You know what is behind "Tommy's invincible gaiety." Let us pray together for a time when the publishing of a book like this will be regarded with fierce shame.

So long and good luck!

Ever yours,

William

Pirbright Huts

1st October, 1915

The day after I had written this letter the news came to me that Robert Whyte had been killed. The letter must stand—I have not the heart to write another. *W.H.L.W.*

CHAPTER 1
Enlisting

At 6.45 p.m. on Saturday, July 25, 1914, Alec and I determined to take part in the Austro-Servian War. I remember the exact minute, because we were standing on the "down" platform of Earl's Court Station, waiting for the 6.55 through train to South Harrow, and Alec had just remarked that we had ten minutes to wait. We had travelled up to London, intending to work in the British Museum for our "vivas" at Oxford, but in the morning it had been so hot that we had strolled round Bloomsbury, smoking our pipes. By lunch-time we had gained such an appetite that we did not feel like work in the afternoon. We went to see Elsie Janis.

The evening papers were full of grave prognostications. War between Servia and Austria seemed inevitable. Earl's Court Station inspired us with the spirit of adventure. We determined to take part, and debated whether we should go out as war correspondents or as orderlies in a Servian hospital. At home we could talk of nothing else during dinner. Ikla, that wisest of all Egyptians, mildly encouraged us, while the family smiled.

On Sunday we learned that war had been declared. Ways and means were discussed, but our great tennis tournament on Monday, and a dance in the evening, left us with a mere background of war-like endeavour. It was vaguely determined that when my "viva" was over we should go and see people of authority in London....

On the last day of July a few of us met together in Gibson's rooms, those neat, white rooms in Balliol that overlook St Giles. Naymier, the Pole, was certain that Armageddon was coming. He proved it conclusively in the Quad with the aid of large maps and a dissertation on potatoes. He also showed us the probable course of the war. We lived in strained excitement. Things were too big to grasp. It was just the other day that 'The Blue Book,' most respectable of Oxford magazines, had published an article showing that a war between Great Britain and Germany was almost unthinkable. It had been written by an undergraduate who had actually been at a German university. Had the multitudinous Anglo-German societies at Oxford worked in vain? The world came crashing round our ears. Naymier was urgent for an Oxford or a Balliol Legion—I do not remember which—but we could not take him seriously. Two of us decided that we were physical cowards, and would not under any circumstances enlist. The flower of Oxford was too valuable to be used as cannon-fodder.

The days passed like weeks. Our minds were hot and confused. It seemed that England must come in. On the afternoon of the fourth of August I travelled up to London. At a certain club in St James's there was little hope. I walked down Pall Mall. In Trafalgar Square a vast, serious crowd was anxiously waiting for news. In Whitehall Belgians were doing their best to rouse the mob. Beflagged cars full of wildly gesticulating Belgians were driving rapidly up and down. Belgians were haranguing little groups of men. Everybody remained quiet but perturbed.

War was a certainty. I did not wish to be a spectator of the scenes that would accompany its declaration, so I went home. All the night in my dreams I saw the quiet, perturbed crowds.

War was declared. All those of us who were at Balliol together telephoned to one another so that we might enlist together. Physical coward or no physical coward—it obviously had to be done. Teddy and Alec were going into the London Scottish. Early in the morning I started for London to join them, but on the way up I read the paragraph in which the War Office appealed for motor-cyclists. So I went straight to Scotland Yard. There I was taken up to a large room full of benches crammed with all sorts and conditions of men. The old fellow on my right was a sign-writer. On my left was a racing motor-cyclist. We waited for hours. Frightened-looking men were sworn in and one phenomenally grave small boy. Later I should have said that a really fine stamp of man was enlisting. Then they seemed to me a shabby crew.

At last we were sent downstairs, and told to strip and array ourselves in moderately dirty blue dressing-gowns. Away from the formality of the other room we sang little songs, and made the worst jokes in the world—being continually interrupted by an irritable sergeant, whom we called "dearie." One or two men were feverishly arguing whether certain physical deficiencies would be passed. Nobody said a word of his reason for enlisting except the sign-writer, whose wages had been low.

The racing motor-cyclist and I were passed one after another, and, receiving warrants, we travelled down to Fulham. Our names, addresses, and qualifications were written down. To my overwhelming joy I was marked as "very suitable." I went to Great Portland Street, arranged to buy a motor-cycle, and returned home. That evening I received a telegram from Oxford advising me to go down to Chatham.

I started off soon after breakfast, and suffered three punctures. The mending of them put despatch-riding in an unhealthy light. At Rochester I picked up Wallace and Marshall of my college, and together we went to the appointed place. There we found twenty or thirty enlisted or unenlisted. I had come only to make inquiries, but I was carried away. After a series of waits I was medically examined and passed. At 5.45 p.m. I kissed the Book, and in two minutes I became a corporal in the Royal Engineers. During the ceremony my chief sensation was one of thoroughgoing panic.

In the morning four of us, who were linguists, were packed off to the War Office. We spent the journey in picturing all the ways we might be killed, until, by the time we reached Victoria, there was not a single one of us who would not have given anything to un-enlist. The War Office rejected us on the plea that they had as many Intelligence Officers as they wanted. So we returned glumly.

The next few days we were drilled, lectured, and given our kit. We began to know each other, and make friends. Finally, several of us, who wanted to go out together, managed by slight misstatements to be put into one batch. We were chosen to join the 5th Division. The Major in command told us—to our great relief—that the Fifth would not form part of the first Expeditionary Force.

I remember Chatham as a place of heat, intolerable dirt, and a bad sore throat. There we made our first acquaintance with the army, which we undergraduates had derided as a crowd of slavish wastrels and empty-headed slackers. We met with tact and courtesy from the mercenary. A sergeant of the Sappers we discovered to be as fine a type of man as any in the wide earth. And we marvelled, too, at the smoothness of organisation, the lack of confusing hurry....

We were to start early on Monday morning. My mother and sister rushed down to Chatham, and my sister has urgently requested me to mention in "the book" that she carried, with much labour, a large and heavy pair of skiing boots. Most of the others had enlisted like myself in a hurry. They did not see "their people" until December.

All of us were made to write our names in the visitors' book, for, as the waiter said—

"They ain't nobodies now, but in these 'ere times yer never knows what they may be."

Then, when we had gone in an ear-breaking splutter of exhausts, he turned to comfort my mother—

"Pore young fellers! Pore young fellers! I wonder if any of 'em will return."

That damp chilly morning I was very sleepy and rather frightened at the new things I was going to do. I imagined war as a desperate continuous series of battles, in which I should ride along the trenches picturesquely haloed with bursting shell, varied by innumerable encounters with Uhlans, or solitary forest rides and immense tiring treks over deserted country to distant armies. I wasn't quite sure I liked the idea of it all. But the sharp morning air, the interest in training a new motor-cycle in the way it should go, the unexpected popping-up and grotesque salutes of wee gnome-like Boy Scouts, soon made me forget the war. A series of the kind of little breakdowns you always have in a collection of new bikes delayed us considerably, and only a race over greasy *setts* through the southern suburbs, over Waterloo Bridge and across the Strand, brought us to Euston just as the boat-train was timed to start. In the importance of our new uniforms we stopped it, of course, and rode joyfully from one end of the platform to the other, much to the agitation of the guard, while I posed delightfully against a bookstall to be photographed by a patriotic governess.

Very grimy we sat down to a marvellous breakfast, and passed the time reading magazines and discussing the length of the war. We put it at from three to six weeks. At Holyhead we carefully took our bikes aboard, and settled down to a cold voyage. We were all a trifle apprehensive at our lack of escort, for then, you will remember, it had not yet been proved how innocuous the German fleet is in our own seas.[1]

Ireland was a disappointment. Everybody was dirty and unfriendly, staring at us with hostile eyes. Add Dublin grease, which beats the Belgian, and a crusty garage proprietor who only after persuasion supplied us with petrol, and you may be sure we were glad to see the last of it. The road to Carlow was bad and bumpy. But the sunset was fine, and we liked the little low Irish cottages in the twilight. When it was quite dark we stopped at a town with a hill in it. One of our men had a brick thrown at him as he rode in, and when we came to the inn we didn't get a gracious word, and decided it was more pleasant not to be a soldier in Ireland. The daughter of the house was pretty and passably clean, but it was very grimly that she had led me through an immense gaudy drawing-room disconsolate in dust wrappings, to a little room where we could wash. She gave us an exiguous meal at an extortionate charge, and refused to put more than two of us up; so, on the advice of two gallivanting lancers who had escaped from the Curragh for some supper, we called in the aid of the police, and were billeted magnificently on the village.

A moderate breakfast at an unearthly hour, a trouble with the starting up of our bikes, and we were off again. It was about nine when we turned into Carlow Barracks.

---

1. This was written before the days of the "Submarine Blockade."

The company sighed with relief on seeing us. We completed the establishment on mobilisation. Our two "artificers," Cecil and Grimers, had already arrived. We were overjoyed to see them. We realised that what they did not know about motor-cycles was not worth knowing, and we had suspected at Chatham what we found afterwards to be true, that no one could have chosen for us pleasanter comrades or more reliable workers.

A fine breakfast was soon prepared for us and we begun looking round. The position should have been a little difficult—a dozen or so 'Varsity men, very fresh from their respective universities, thrown as corporals at the head of a company of professional soldiers. We were determined that, whatever vices we might have, we should not be accused of "swank." The sergeants, after a trifle of preliminary stiffness, treated us with fatherly kindness, and did all they could to make us comfortable and teach us what we wanted to learn.

Carlow was a fascinating little town. The National Volunteers still drilled just behind the barracks. It was not wise to refer to the Borderers or to Ulster, but the war had made all the difference in the world. We were to represent Carlow in the Great War. Right through the winter Carlow never forgot us. They sent us comforts and cigarettes and Christmas Puddings. When the 5th Signal Company returns, Carlow will go mad.

My first "official" ride was to Dublin. It rained most of the way there and all the way back, but a glow of patriotism kept me warm. In Dublin I went into a little public-house for some beer and bread and cheese. The landlord told me that though he wasn't exactly a lover of soldiers, things had changed now. On my return I was given lunch in the Officers' Mess, for nobody could consider their men more than the officers of our company.

The next day we were inoculated. At the time we would much rather have risked typhoid. We did not object to the discomfort, though two of us nearly fainted on parade the following morning—it was streamingly hot—but our farewell dinner was absolutely spoilt. Bottles of the best Moselle Carlow could produce were left untouched. Songs broke down in curses. It was tragic.

CHAPTER 2

The Journey to the Front

We made a triumphant departure from Carlow, preceded down to the station by the band of the N.V. We were told off to prevent anybody entering the station, but all the men entered magnificently, saying they were volunteers, and the women and children rushed us with the victorious cry, "We've downed the p'lice." We steamed out of the station while the band played "Come back to Erin" and "God save Ireland," and made an interminable journey to Dublin. At some of the villages they cheered, at others they looked at us glumly. But the back streets of Dublin were patriotic enough, and at the docks, which we reached just after dark, a small, tremendously enthusiastic crowd was gathered to see us off.

They sang songs and cheered, and cheered and sang songs. "I can generally bear the separation, but I don't like the leave-taking." The boat would not go off. The crowd on the boat and the crowd on the wharf made patriotic noises until they were hoarse. At midnight our supporters had nearly all gone away. We who had seen our motor-cycles carefully hoisted on board ate the buns and apples provided by "Friends in Dublin" and chatted. A young gunner told me of all his amours, and they were very numerous. Still—

For my uncle Toby's amours running all the way in my head, they had the same effect upon me as if they had been my own—I was in the most perfect state of bounty and goodwill—

So I set about finding a place for sleep.

The whole of the Divisional Headquarters Staff, with all

their horses, were on the *Archimedes*, and we were so packed that when I tried to find a place to sleep I discovered there was not an inch of space left on the deck, so I passed an uncomfortable night on top of some excruciatingly hard ropes.

We cast off about one in the morning. The night was horribly cold, and a slow dawn was never more welcomed. But day brought a new horror. The sun poured down on us, and the smell from the horses packed closely below was almost unbearable; while, worst of all, we had to go below to wash and to draw our rations.

Then I was first introduced to bully. The first tin tastes delicious and fills you rapidly. You never actually grow to dislike it, and many times when extra hungry I have longed for an extra tin. But when you have lived on bully for three months (we have not been served out with fresh meat more than a dozen times altogether),[2] how you long for any little luxuries to vary the monotony of your food!

On the morning of the third day we passed a French destroyer with a small prize in tow, and rejoiced greatly, and towards evening we dropped anchor off Havre. On either side of the narrow entrance to the docks there were cheering crowds, and we cheered back, thrilled, occasionally breaking into the soldier's anthem, "It's a long, long way to Tipperary."[3]

We disembarked at a secluded wharf, and after waiting about for a couple of hours or so—we had not then learned to wait—we were marched off to a huge dim warehouse, where we were given gallons of the most delicious hot coffee, and bought scrumptious little cakes.

It was now quite dark, and, for what seemed whole nights, we sat wearily waiting while the horses were taken off the transport. We made one vain dash for our quarters, but found only another enormous warehouse, strangely lit, full of clattering wagons and restive horses. We watched with wonder a battery clank out into the night, and then returned sleepily to the wharf-side. Very late

---

2. This was written in the middle of October.

3. We became bored with the song, and dropped it soon after for less printable songs.

we found where we were to sleep, a gigantic series of wool warehouses. The warehouses were full of wool and the wool was full of fleas. We were very miserable, and a little bread and wine we managed to get hold of hardly cheered us at all. I feared the fleas, and spread a waterproof sheet on the bare stones outside. I thought I should not get a wink of sleep on such a Jacobean resting-place, but, as a matter of fact, I slept like a top, and woke in the morning without even an ache. But those who had risked the wool——!

We breakfasted off the strong, sweet tea that I have grown to like so much, and some bread, butter, and chocolate we bought off a smiling old woman at the warehouse gates. Later in the morning we were allowed into the town. First, a couple of us went into a café to have a drink, and when we came out we found our motor-cycles garlanded with flowers by two admiring flappers. Everywhere we went we were the gods of a very proper worship, though the shopkeepers in their admiration did not forget to charge. We spent a long, lazy day in lounging through the town, eating a lot of little meals and in visiting the public baths—the last bath I was to have, if I had only known it, for a month. A cheery, little, bustling town Havre seemed to us, basking in a bright sunshine, and the hopes of our early overwhelming victory. We all stalked about, prospective conquerors, and talked fluently of the many defects of the German army.

Orders came in the afternoon that we were to move that night. I sat up until twelve, and gained as my reward some excellent hot tea and a bit of rather tough steak. At twelve everybody was woken up and the company got ready to move. We motor-cyclists were sent off to the station. Foolishly I went by myself. Just outside what I thought was the station I ran out of petrol. I walked to the station and waited for the others. They did not come. I searched the station, but found nothing except a cavalry brigade entraining. I rushed about feverishly. There was no one I knew, no one who had heard anything of my company. Then I grew horribly frightened that I should be left behind. I pelted back to the old warehouses, but found everybody had left two hours ago. I thought the company must surely have gone by now, and started in my desperation asking everybody I knew if they had seen anything of the company. Luckily I came across an entraining officer, who told me that the company were entraining at "Point Six-Hangar de Laine,"—three miles away. I simply ran there, asking my way of surly, sleepy sentries, tripping over ropes, nearly falling into docks.

I found the Signal Company. There was not a sign of our train. So Johnson took me on his carrier back to the station I had searched in such fear. We found the motor-cycle, Johnson gave me some petrol, and we returned to Point Six. It was dawn when the old train at last rumbled and squeaked into the siding.

I do not know how long we took to entrain, I was so sleepy. But the sun was just rising when the little trumpet shrilled, the long train creaked over the points, and we woke for a moment to murmur—By Jove, we're off now—and I whispered thankfully to myself—Thank heaven I found them at last.

We were lucky enough to be only six in our compartment, but, as you know, in a French 3rd class there is very little room, while the seats are fiercely hard. And we had not yet been served out with blankets. Still, we had to stick it for twenty-four hours. Luckily the train stopped at every station of any importance, so, taking the law into our own hands, we got out and stretched our legs at every opportunity.

We travelled *viâ* Rouen and Amiens to Landrecies. The Signal Company had a train to itself. Gradually we woke up to find ourselves travelling through extraordinarily pretty country and cheering crowds. At each level-crossing the *curé* was there to bless us. If we did not stop the people threw in fruit, which we vainly endeavoured to catch. A halt, and they were round us, beseeching us for souvenirs, loading us with fruit, and making us feel that it was a fine thing to fight in a friendly country.

At Rouen we drew up at a siding, and sent porters scurrying for bread and butter and beer, while we loaded up from women who came down to the train with all sorts of delicious little cakes and sweets. We stopped, and then rumbled slowly towards Amiens. At St Roche we first saw wounded, and heard, I do not know with what truth, that four aviators had been killed,

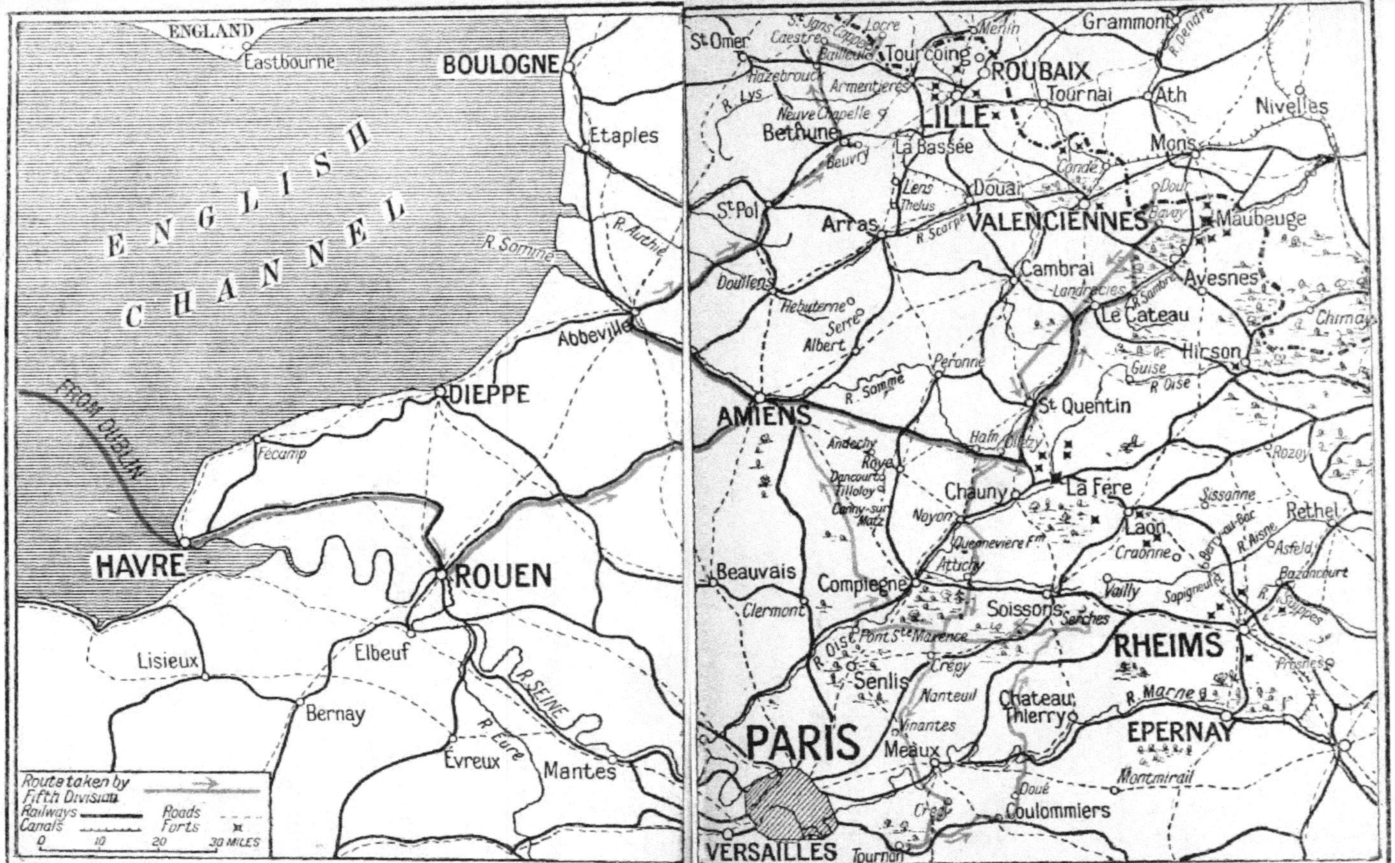
ENGLAND
Eastbourne
ENGLISH CHANNEL
FROM DUBLIN
BOULOGNE
Etaples
R. Somme
R. Authie
Abbeville
DIEPPE
Fecamp
HAVRE
ROUEN
Lisieux
Elbeuf
Bernay
Evreux
R. Eure
R. SEINE
Mantes
Route taken by Fifth Division
Railways
Canals
Roads
Forts
0 10 20 30 MILES
St Omer
Hazebrouck
R. Lys
Armentières
Tourcoing
ROUBAIX
LILLE
Tournai
Ath
Grammont
Nivelles
Bethune
La Bassée
Mons
St Pol
Arras
Douai
Lens
VALENCIENNES
Maubeuge
Cambrai
Avesnes
Le Cateau
Doullens
Albert
Chimay
Hirson
Peronne
AMIENS
St Quentin
Guise
R. Oise
Chauny
La Fere
Noyon
Laon
Rethel
Beauvais
Compiegne
Soissons
Vailly
Craonne
Clermont
Senlis
RHEIMS
Chateau Thierry
PARIS
Meaux
EPERNAY
R. Marne
Coulommiers
Montmirail
VERSAILLES
Tournan

and that our General, Grierson, had died of heart failure. At Ham they measured me against a lamp-post, and ceremoniously marked the place. The next time I passed through Ham I had no time to look for the mark! It began to grow dark, and the trees standing out against the sunset reminded me of our two lines of trees at home. We went slowly over bridges, and looked fearfully from our windows for bursting shells. Soon we fell asleep, and were wakened about midnight by shouted orders. We had arrived at Landrecies, near enough the Frontier to excite us.

I wonder if you realise at home what the Frontier meant to us at first? We conceived it as a thing guarded everywhere by intermittent patrols of men staring carefully towards Germany and Belgium in the darkness, a thing to be defended at all costs, at all times, to be crossed with triumph and recrossed with shame. We did not understand what an enormous, incredible thing modern war was—how it cared nothing for frontiers, or nations, or people.

Very wearily we unloaded our motor bicycles and walked to the barracks, where we put down our kit and literally feel asleep, to be wakened for fatigue work.

We rose at dawn, and had some coffee at a little *estaminet*,[4] where a middle-aged dame, horribly arch, cleaned my canteen for me, *pour l'amour de toi*. We managed an excellent breakfast of bacon and eggs before establishing the Signal Office at the barracks. A few of us rode off to keep touch with the various brigades that were billeted round. The rest of us spent the morning across the road at an inn drinking much wine-and-water and planning out the war on a forty-year-old map.

In the afternoon I went out with two others to prospect some roads, very importantly. We were rather annoyed to lose our way out of the town, and were very short with some inquisitive small boys who stood looking over our shoulders as we squatted on the grass by the wayside studying our maps.

We had some tea at a mad village called Hecq. All the inhabitants were old, ugly, smelly, and dirty; and they crowded round us as we devoured a magnificent omelette, endeavouring to in-

4. The word used in Flanders for a tavern that does not aspire to the dignity of "restaurant" or "hotel."

cite us to do all sorts of things to the German women if ever we reached Germany. We returned home in the late afternoon to hear rumours of an advance next day.

Three of us wandered into the Square to have a drink. There I first tried a new pipe that had been given me. The one pipe I brought with me I had dropped out of the train between Amiens and Landrecies. It had been quite a little tragedy, as it was a pipe for which I had a great affection. It had been my companion in Switzerland and Paris.

Coming back from the Square I came across an excited crowd. It appears that an inoffensive, rather buxom-looking woman had been walking round the Square when one of her breasts cooed and flew away. We shot three spies at Landrecies.

I hung round the Signal Office, nervous and excited, for "a run." The night was alive with the tramp of troops and the rumble of guns. The old 108th passed by—huge good-natured guns, each drawn by eight gigantic plough-horses. I wonder if you can understand—the thrilling excitement of waiting and listening by night in a town full of troops.

At midnight I took my first despatch. It was a dark, starless night; very misty on the road. From the brigade I was sent on to an ambulance—an unpleasant ride, because, apart from the mist and the darkness, I was stopped every few yards by sentries of the West Kents, a regiment which has now about the best reputation of any battalion out here. I returned in time to snatch a couple of hours of sleep before we started at dawn for Belgium.

When the Division moves we ride either with the column or go in advance to the halting-place. That morning we rode with the column, which meant riding three-quarters of a mile or so and then waiting for the main-guard to come up—an extraordinarily tiring method of getting along.

The day (August 21) was very hot indeed, and the troops who had not yet got their marching feet suffered terribly, even though the people by the wayside brought out fruit and eggs and drinks. There was murmuring when some officers refused to allow their men to accept these gifts. But a start had to be made some time, for promiscuous drinks do not increase marching efficiency. We, of course, could do pretty well what we liked. A little coffee early in the morning, and then anything we cared to ask for. Most of us in the evening discovered, unpleasantly enough, forgotten pears in unthought-of pockets.

About 1.30 we neared Bavai, and I was sent on to find out about billeting arrangements, but by the time they were completed the rest had arrived.

For a long time we were hutted in the Square. Spuggy found a "friend," and together we obtained a good wash. The people were vociferously enthusiastic. Even the chemist gave us some "salts" free of charge.

My first ride from Bavai began with a failure, as, owing to belt-slip, I endeavoured vainly to start for half an hour (or so it seemed) in the midst of an interested but sympathetic populace. A smart change saw me tearing along the road to meet with a narrow escape from untimely death in the form of a car, which I tried to pass on the wrong side. In the evening we received our first batch of pay, and dining magnificently at a hotel, took tearful leave of Huggie and Spuggy. They had been chosen, they said, to make a wild dash through to Liége. We speculated darkly on their probable fate. In the morning we learned that we had been hoaxed, and used suitable language.

We slept uncomfortably on straw in a back yard, and rose again just before dawn. We breakfasted hastily at a café, and were off just as the sun had risen.

Our day's march was to Dour, in Belgium, and for us a bad day's march it was. My job was to keep touch with the 14th Brigade, which was advancing along a parallel road to the west.[5] That meant riding four or five miles across rough country roads, endeavouring to time myself so as to reach the 14th column just when the S.O. was passing, then back again to the Division, riding up and down the column until I found our captain. In the course of my riding that day I knocked down "a civvy" in Dour, and bent a foot-rest endeavouring to avoid a major, but that was all in the day's work.

The Signal Office was first established patriarchally with a

5. The Bavai-Andregnies-Elouges road.

table by the roadside, and thence I made my last journey that day to the 14th. I found them in a village under the most embarrassing attentions. As for myself, while I was waiting, a *curé* photographed me, a woman rushed out and washed my face, and children crowded up to me, presenting me with chocolate and cigars, fruit and eggs, until my haversack was practically bursting.

When I returned I found the S.O. had shifted to the station of Dour. We were given the waiting-room, which we made comfortable with straw. Opposite the station was a hotel where the Staff lived. It was managed by a curiously upright old man in a threadbare frock-coat, bright check trousers, and carpet slippers. Nadine, his pretty daughter, was tremulously eager to make us comfortable, and the two days we were at Dour we hung round the hotel, sandwiching omelettes and drink between our despatches.

Chapter 3

The Battle of Mons

We knew nothing of what was going on. There was a rumour that Namur had fallen, and I heard certain officers say we had advanced dangerously far. The cavalry was on our left and the Third Division on our right. Beyond the Third Division we had heard of the First Corps, but nothing of the French. We were left, to the best of our knowledge, a tenuous bulwark against the German hosts.

The 14th Brigade had advanced by the Andregnies road to Elouges and the Canal. The 13th was our right brigade, and the 15th, at first in reserve, extended our line on the second day to Frameries. The Cyclists were reconnoitring north of the Canal.

The roads round Dour were of the very worst *pavé*, and, if this were not enough, the few maps we had between us were useless. The villages of Waasmes, Paturages, and Frameries were in the midst of such a network of roads that the map could not possibly be clear. If the country had been flat, we might at least have found our way by landmarks. It was not. The roads wandered round great slag-heaps, lost themselves in little valleys, ran into pits and groups of buildings. Each one tried to be exactly like all its fellows. Without a map to get from Elouges to Frameries was like asking an American to make his way from Richmond Park to Denmark Hill.

About ten o'clock on the morning of August 23rd I was sent out to find General Gleichen, who was reported somewhere near Waasmes. I went over nightmare roads, uneven cobbles with great pits in them. I found him, and was told by him to tell the General that the position was unfortunate owing to a weak salient. We had already heard guns, but on my way back I heard a distant crash, and looked round to find that a shell had burst half a mile away on a slag-heap, between Dour and myself. With my heart thumping against my ribs I opened the throttle, until I was jumping at 40 m.p.h. from cobble to cobble. Then, realising that I was in far greater danger of breaking my neck than of being shot, I pulled myself together and slowed down to proceed sedately home.

The second time I went out to General Gleichen I found him a little farther back from his former position. This time he was on the railway. While I was waiting for a reply we had an excellent view of German guns endeavouring to bring down one of our aeroplanes. So little did we know of aeroplanes then, that the General was persuaded by his brigade-major to step back into shelter from the falling bits, and we all stared anxiously skywards, expecting every moment that our devoted aviator would be hit.

That evening Huggie and I rode back to Bavai and beyond in search of an errant ammunition column. Eventually we found it and brought news of it back to H.Q. I shall never forget the captain reading my despatch by the light of my lamp, the wagons guarded by Dorsets with fixed bayonets appearing to disappear shadowy in the darkness. We showed the captain a short-cut that avoided Bavai, then left him. His horses were tired, but he was forced to push them on another ten miles to Dour. We got back at 10, and found Nadine weeping. We questioned her, but she would not tell us why.

There was a great battle very early the next morning, a running-about and set, anxious faces. We were all sent off in rapid succession. I was up early and managed to get a wash at the station-master's house, his wife providing me with coffee, which, much to my discomfiture, she liberally dosed with rum. At 6.30 Johnson started on a message to the 15th Brigade. We never saw him again. At 9.15 three despatch riders who had gone to the 15th, George, Johnson, and Grimers, had not returned. I was sent. Two miles out I met George with Grimers' despatches. Neither of them had been able to find the 15th. I took the despatches and sent George back to report. I went down a road, which I calculated ought to bring me somewhere on the left of the 15th, who were supposed to be somewhere between Paturages and Frameries. There were two villages on hills, one on each side. I struck into the north end of the village on my left; there was no road to the one on my right.[6] I came across a lot of disheartened stragglers retreating up the hill. I went a little farther and saw our own firing line a quarter of a mile ahead. There was a bit of shrapnel flying about, but not much. I struck back up the hill and came upon a crowd of fugitive infantry men, all belonging to the 13th Brigade. At last I found General Cuthbert, the Brigadier of the 13th, sitting calmly on his horse watching the men pass. I asked him where the 15th was. He did not know, but told me significantly that our rallying-point was Athis.

I rode a little farther, and came upon his signal officer. He stopped me and gave me a verbal message to the General, telling me that the 15th appeared to be cut off. As I had a verbal message to take back there was no need for me to go farther with my despatches, which, as it appeared later, was just as well. I sprinted back to Dour, picking my way through a straggling column of men sullenly retreating. At the station I found everybody packing up. The General received my message without a word, except one of thanks.

The right flank of the 13th has been badly turned.

Most of our officers have been killed.

Some companies of the K.O.S.B. are endeavouring to cover our retreat.

We viciously smashed all the telegraph instruments in the office and cut all the wires. It took me some time to pack up my kit and tie it on my carrier. When I had finished, everybody had gone. I could hear their horses clattering up the street. Across the way Nadine stood weeping. A few women with glazed, resigned eyes, stood listlessly round her. Behind me, I heard the

6. I had no map with me. All the maps were in use. Looking afterwards at the map which I obtained later in the day, I am unable to trace my route with any accuracy. It is certain that the Germans temporarily thrust in a wedge between the 13th and 15th Brigades.

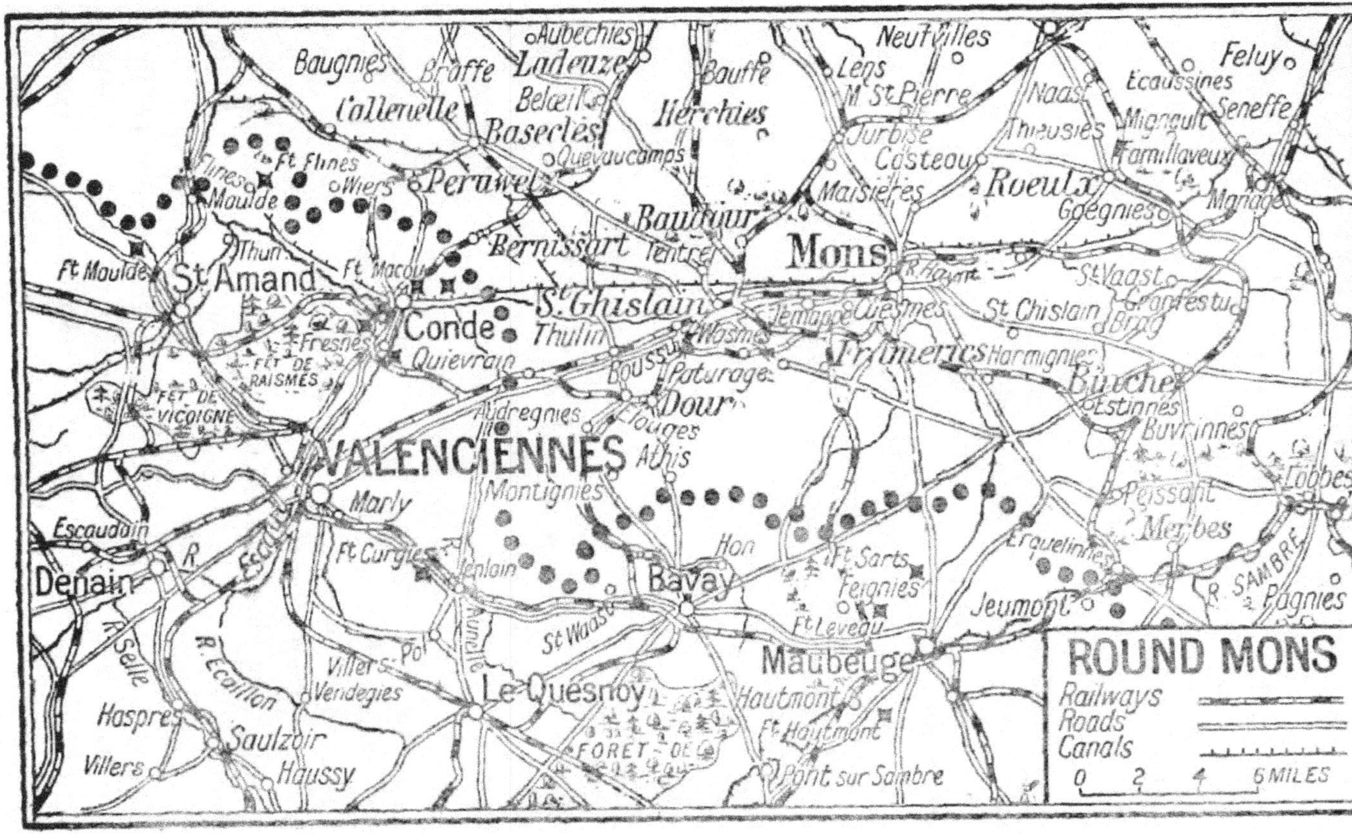
ROUND MONS
Railways
Roads
Canals
0 2 4 6 MILES
Mons
VALENCIENNES
St Amand
Conde
St Ghislain
Bavay
Maubeuge
Le Quesnoy
Denain
Binche
Roeulx
Peruwelz
Bernissart
Baudour
Frameries
Dour
Boussu
Paturage
Wasmes
Quievrain
Thulin
Jemappe
Quesmes
Harmignies
St Ghislain
Bray
St Vaast
Estinnes
Buvrinnes
Lobbes
Peissant
Merbes
Erquelinnes
Jeumont
R. Sambre
Pagnies
Hon
Ft Sarts
Feignies
Ft Leveau
Hautmont
Ft Hautmont
Pont sur Sambre
Foret de
St Waast
Villers Pol
Vendegies
Jenlain
Ft Curgies
Marly
Montignies
Athis
Elouges
Audregnies
Escaudain
R. Selle
R. Ecaillon
Haspres
Saulzoir
Villers
Haussy
Ft Maulde
Maulde
Flines
Ft Flines
Wiers
Thun
Ft Macou
Fresnes
Fet de Raismes
Fet de Vicoigne
Baugnies
Braffe
Callenelle
Aubechies
Ladeuze
Beloeil
Basecles
Quevaucamps
Bauffe
Herchies
Neufvilles
Lens
Mt St Pierre
Jurbise
Casteau
Maisières
Naast
Thieusies
Goegnies
Ecaussines
Mignault
Familleureux
Seneffe
Feluy
Manage

first shell crash dully into the far end of the town. It seemed to me I could not just go off. So I went across to Nadine and muttered *"Nous reviendrons, Mademoiselle."* But she would not look at me, so I jumped on my bicycle, and with a last glance round at the wrecked, deserted station, I rode off, shouting to encourage more myself than the others, *"Ça va bien."*

I caught up the General, and passed him to ride on ahead of the Signal Company. Never before had I so wished my engine to turn more slowly. It seemed a shame that we motor-cyclists should head the retreat of our little column. I could not understand how the men could laugh and joke. It was blasphemous. They ought to be cursing with angry faces—at the least, to be grave and sorrowful.

I was told that Divisional Headquarters would be established at Villers-Pol, a little country village about ten miles west of Bavai and eight miles south-east of Valenciennes. I rode to St Waast, a few miles out of Bavai, and, finding there a cavalry colonel (of the 2nd Life Guards, I think), gave him all the news. I hurried on to Jenlain, thinking I might be of some use to the troops on our right flank, but Jenlain was peaceful and empty. So I cut across low rolling downs to Villers-Pol. There was nobody there when I arrived. The sun was shining very brightly. Old women were sleeping at the doors; children were playing lazily on the road. Soon one or two motor-cyclists dribbled in, and about an hour later a section of the Signal Company arrived after a risky dash along country lanes. They outspanned, and we, as always, made for the inn.

There was a mother in the big room. She was a handsome little woman of about twenty-four. Her husband was at the war. She asked me why we had come to Villers-Pol. I said we were retreating a little—*pour attaquer le mieux—un mouvement stratégique.* She wept bitterly and loudly, "Ah, my baby, what will they do to us? They will kill you, and they will ill-treat me so that never again shall I be able to look my husband in the eyes—his brave eyes; but now perhaps they are closed in death!"

There was an older, harsh-featured woman who rated the mother for her silliness, and, while we ate our omelette, the room was filled with the clamour of them until a dog outside began to howl. Then the mother went and sat down in a chair by the fire and stopped crying, but every now and then moaned and clasped her baby strongly to her breast, murmuring, "My poor baby, my poor baby, what shall we do?"

We lounged about the place until a cavalry brigade came through. The General commandeered me to find his transport. This I did, and on the way back waited for the brigade to pass. Then for the first time I saw that many riderless horses were being led, that some of the horses and many of the men were wounded, and that one regiment of lancers was pathetically small. It was the 2nd Cavalry Brigade, that had charged the enemy's guns, to find them protected by barbed wire.

Sick at heart I rode back into Villers-Pol, and found the Signal Company hastily harnessing up. Headquarters had been compelled to go farther back still—to St Waast, and there was nobody, so far as we knew, between us and the Germans. The order caught George with his gear down. We made a marvellously rapid repair, then went off at the trot. A mile out, and I was sent back to pick up our quartermaster and three others who were supposed to have been left behind. It was now quite dark. In the village I could not find our men, but discovered a field ambulance that did not know what to do. Their horses were dead tired, but I advised them strongly to get on. They took my advice, and I heard at Serches that they left Villers-Pol as the Germans[7] entered it. They were pursued, but somehow got away in the darkness.

I went on, and at some cross-roads in a black forest came across a regiment of hussars. I told them where their B.H.Q. was, and their Colonel muttered resignedly,

"It's a long way, but we shall never get our wounded horses there to-morrow." I put two more companies right, then came across a little body of men who were vainly trying to get a horse attached to a S.A.A. limber out of the ditch. It was a pitch-black night, and they were bravely endeavouring to do it without catching a glimpse of the horse. I gave them the benefit of

7. A small patrol of cavalry, I should imagine, if the tale I heard at Serches be true.

my lamp until they had got the brute out. Two more bodies of stragglers I directed, and then pushed on rapidly to St Waast, where I found all the other motor-cyclists safe except Johnson. Two had come on carts, having been compelled to abandon their motor-cycles.

George had been attached to the 14th. He had gone with them to the canal, and had been left there with the Cornwalls when the 14th had retired to its second position. At last nobody remained with him except a section. They were together in a hut, and outside he could hear the bullets singing. He noticed some queer-looking explosives in a corner, and asked what they were for. He was told they were to blow up the bridge over the canal, so decided it was time for him to quit, and did so with some rapidity under a considerable rifle fire. Then he was sent up to the Manchesters, who were holding a ready-made trench across the main road. As he rode up he tells me men shouted at him, "Don't go that way, it's dangerous," until he grew quite frightened; but he managed to get to the trench all right, slipped in, and was shown how to crawl along until he reached the colonel.

N'Soon and Sadders were with the 13th. On the Sunday night they had to march to a new position more towards their right. The Signal Section went astray and remained silently on a byroad while their officer reconnoitred. On the main road between them and their lines were some lights rapidly moving—Germans in armoured motor-cars. They successfully rejoined, but in the morning there was something of a collision, and Sadders' bicycle was finished. He got hold of a push-bike alongside the wagons for some distance, finishing up on a limber.

Spuggy was sent up to the trenches in the morning. He was under heavy shell fire when his engine seized up. His brigade was retreating, and he was in the rear of it, so, leaving his bicycle, he took to his heels, and with the Germans in sight ran till he caught up a wagon. He clambered on, and so came into St Waast.

I had not been in many minutes when I was sent off to our Army H.Q. at Bavai. It was a miserable ride. I was very tired, the road was full of transport, and my lamp would not give more than a feeble glimmer.

I got to bed at 1 a.m. About 3.30 (on August 24) I was called and detailed to remain with the rear-guard. First I was sent off to find the exact position of various bodies posted on roads to stem the German advance. At one spot I just missed a shell-trap. A few minutes after I had left, some of the Manchesters, together with a body of the D. Cyclists who were stationed three miles or so out of St Waast, were attacked by a body of Jaegers, who appeared on a hill opposite. Foolishly they disclosed their position by opening rifle fire. In a few minutes the Jaegers went, and to our utter discomfiture a couple of field-guns appeared and fired point-blank at 750 yards. Luckily the range was not very exact, and only a few were wounded—those who retired directly backwards instead of transversely out of the shells' direction.

The H.Q. of the rear-guard left St Waast about 5.30. It was cold and chilly. What happened I do not quite know. All I remember was that at a given order a battery would gallop off the road into action against an enemy we could not see. So to Bavai, where I was sent off with an important despatch for D.H.Q. I had to ride past the column, and scarcely had I gone half a mile when my back tyre burst. There was no time to repair it, so on I bumped, slipping all over the road. At D.H.Q., which of course was on the road, I borrowed some one else's bicycle and rode back by another road. On the way I came across Huggie filling up from an abandoned motor-lorry. I did likewise, and then tore into Bavai. A shell or two was bursting over the town, and I was nearly slaughtered by some infantrymen, who thought they were firing at an aeroplane. Dodging their bullets, I left the town, and eventually caught up the H.Q. of the rear-guard.

It was now about 10.30. Until five the troops tramped on, in a scorching sun, on roads covered with clouds of dust. And most pitiful of all, between the rear-guard and the main body shuffled the wounded; for we had been forced to evacuate our hospital at Bavai. Our men were mad at retreating. The Germans had advanced on them in the closest order. Each fellow firmly believed he had killed fifty, and was perfectly certain we could have held our line to the crack of doom. They trudged and trudged. The women, who had cheerily given us everything a few days before, now with anxious faces timorously offered us water and fruit.

Great ox-wagons full of refugees, all in their best clothes, came in from side-roads. None of them were allowed on the roads we were retreating along, so I suppose they were pushed across the German front until they fell into the Germans' hands.

For us it was column-riding the whole day—half a mile or so, and then a halt—heart-breaking work.

I was riding along more or less by myself in a gap that had been left in the column. A *curé* stopped me. He was a very tall and very thin young man with a hasty, frightened manner. Behind him was a flock of panic-stricken, chattering old women. He asked me if there was any danger. Not that he was afraid, he said, but just to satisfy his people. I answered that none of them need trouble to move. I was too ashamed to say we were retreating, and I had an eye on the congestion of the roads. I have sometimes wondered what that tall, thin *curé*, with the sallow face and the frightened eyes, said about me when, not twelve hours later, the German advance-guard triumphantly defiled before him.

Late in the afternoon we passed through Le Cateau, a bright little town, and came to the village of Reumont, where we were billeted in a large barn.

We were all very confident that evening. We heard that we were holding a finely entrenched position, and the General made a speech—I did not hear it—in which he told us that there had been a great Russian success, and that in the battle of the morrow a victory for us would smash the Germans once and for all. But our captain was more pessimistic. He thought we should suffer a great disaster. Doubting, we snuggled down in the straw, and went soundly to sleep.

CHAPTER 4

The Battle of Le Cateau

The principal thing about Le Cateau is that the soldiers pronounce it to rhyme with Waterloo—Leacatoo—and all firmly believe that if the French cavalry had come up to help us, as the Prussians came up at Waterloo, there would have been no Germans to fight against us now.

It was a cold misty morning when we awoke, but later the day was fine enough. We got up, had a cheery and exiguous breakfast to distant, intermittent firing, then did a little work on our bicycles. I spent an hour or so watching through glasses the dim movement of dull bodies of troops and shrapnel bursting vaguely on the horizon. Then we were all summoned to H.Q., which were stationed about a mile out from Reumont on the Le Cateau road. In front of us the road dipped sharply and rose again over the brow of a hill about two miles away. On this brow, stretching right and left of the road, there was a line of poplars. On the slope of the hill nearer to us there were two or three field batteries in action. To the right of us a brigade of artillery was limbered up ready to go anywhere. In the left, at the bottom of the dip the 108th was in action, partially covered by some sparse bushes. A few ambulance wagons and some miscellaneous first-line transport were drawn up along the side of the road at the bottom of the dip. To the N.W. we could see for about four miles over low, rolling fields. We could see nothing to the right, as our view was blocked by a cottage and some trees and hedges. On the roof of the cottage a wooden platform had been made. On it stood the General and his Chief of Staff and our Captain.

Four telephone operators worked for their lives in pits breast-high, two on each side of the road. The Signal Clerk sat at a table behind the cottage, while round him, or near him, were the motor-cyclists and cyclists.

About the battle itself you know as much as I. We had wires out to all the brigades, and along them the news would come and orders would go.

The —— are holding their position satisfactorily.

Our flank is being turned.

Should be very grateful for another battalion.

We are under very heavy shell fire.

Right through the battle I did not take a single message. Huggie took a despatch to the 13th, and returned under very heavy shrapnel fire, and for this was very properly mentioned in despatches.

How the battle fluctuated I cannot now remember. But I can still see those poplars almost hidden in the smoke of shrapnel. I can still hear the festive crash of the Heavies as they fired slowly, scientifically, and well. From 9 to 12.30 we remained there kicking our heels, feverishly calm, cracking the absurdest jokes. Then the word went round that on our left things were going very badly. Two battalions were hurried across, and then, of course, the attack developed even more fiercely on our right.

Wounded began to come through—none groaning, but just men with their eyes clenched and great crimson bandages.

An order was sent to the transport to clear back off the road. There was a momentary panic. The wagons came through at the gallop and with them some frightened foot-sloggers, hanging on and running for dear life. Wounded men from the firing line told us that the shrapnel was unbearable in the trenches.

A man came galloping up wildly from the Heavies. They had run out of fuses. Already we had sent urgent messages to the ammunition lorries, but the road was blocked and they could not get up to us. So Grimers was sent off with a haversack—mine—to fetch fuses and hurry up the lorries. How he got there and back in the time that he did, with the traffic that there was, I cannot even now understand.

It was now about two o'clock, and every moment the news that we heard grew worse and worse, while the wounded poured past us in a continuous stream. I gave my water-bottle to one man who was moaning for water. A horse came galloping along. Across the saddle-bow was a man with a bloody scrap of trouser instead of a leg, while the rider, who had been badly wounded in the arm, was swaying from side to side.

A quarter of an hour before the brigade on our right front had gone into action on the crest of the hill. Now they streamed back at the trot, all telling the tale—how, before they could even unlimber, shells had come crashing into them. The column was a lingering tragedy. There were teams with only a limber and without a gun. And you must see it to know what a twistedly pathetic thing a gun team and limber without a gun is. There were bits of teams and teams with only a couple of drivers. The faces of the men were awful. I smiled at one or two, but they shook their heads and turned away. One sergeant as he passed was muttering to himself, as if he were repeating something over and over again so as to learn it by rote—"My gun, my gun, my gun!"

At this moment an order came from some one for the motor-cyclists to retire to the farm where we had slept the night. The others went on with the crowd, but I could not start my engine. After trying for five minutes it seemed to me absurd to retreat, so I went back and found that apparently nobody had given the order. The other motor-cyclists returned one by one as soon as they could get clear, but most of them were carried on right past the farm.

A few minutes later there was a great screaming crash overhead—shrapnel. I ran to my bicycle and stood by waiting for orders.

The General suggested mildly that we might change our headquarters. There was a second crash. We all retired about 200 yards back up the road. There I went to the captain in the middle of the traffic and asked him what I should do. He told us to get out of it as we could not do anything more—"You have all done magnificently"—then he gave me some messages for our subaltern. I shouted, "So long, sir," and left him, not knowing whether I should ever see him again. I heard afterwards that he went back when all the operators had fled and tried to get into communication with our Army H.Q.

Just as I had started up my engine another shell burst about 100 yards to the left, and a moment later a big wagon drawn by two maddened horses came dashing down into the main street. They could not turn, so went straight into the wall of a house opposite. There was a dull crash and a squirming heap piled up at the edge of the road.

I pushed through the traffic a little and came upon a captain and a subaltern making their way desperately back. I do not know who they were, but I heard a scrap of what they said—

"We must get back for it," said the captain.

"We shall never return," replied the subaltern gravely.

"It doesn't matter," said the captain.

"It doesn't matter," echoed the subaltern.

But I do not think the gun could have been saved.

About six of us collected in a little bunch at the side of the road. On our left we saw a line of infantry running. The road itself was impassable. So we determined to strike off to the right. I led the way, and though we had not the remotest conception whether we should meet British or German, we eventually found our way to 2nd Corps H.Q.

I have only a dim remembrance of what happened there. I went into the signal-office and reported that, so far as I knew, the 5th Division was in flight along the Reumont-Saint-Quentin road.

The sergeant in charge of the 2nd Corps Motor-cyclists offered us some hard-boiled eggs and put me in charge of our lot. Then off we went, and hitting the main road just ahead of our muddled column, halted at the desolate little village of Estrées.

It now began to rain.

Soon the column came pouring past, so miserably and so slowly—lorries, transport, guns, limbers, small batches of infantrymen, crowds of stragglers. All were cursing the French, for right through the battle we had expected the French to come up on our right wing. There had been a whole corps of cavalry a few miles away, but in reply to our urgent request for help their general had reported that his horses were too tired. How we cursed them and cursed them.

After a weary hour's wait our subaltern came up, and, at my request, sent me to look for the captain. I found him about two miles this side of Reumont, endeavouring vainly to make some sort of ordered procession out of the almost comically patchwork medley. Later I heard that the last four hundred yards of the column had been shelled to destruction as it was leaving Reumont, and a tale is told—probably without truth—of an officer shooting the driver of the leading motor-lorry in a hopeless endeavour to get some ammunition into the firing line.

I scooted back and told the others that our captain was still alive, and a little later we pushed off into the flood. It was now getting dark, and the rain, which had held off for a little, was pouring down.

Finally, we halted at a tiny cottage, and the Signal Company outspanned.

We tried to make ourselves comfortable in the wet by hiding under damp straw and putting on all available bits of clothing. But soon we were all soaked to the skin, and it was so dark that horses wandered perilously near. One hungry mare started eating the straw that was covering my chest. That was enough. Desperately we got up to look round for some shelter, and George, our champion "scrounger," discovered a chicken-house. It is true there were nineteen fowls in it. They died a silent and, I hope, a painless death.

The order came round that the motor-cyclists were to spend the night at the cottage—the roads were utterly and hopelessly impassable—while the rest of the company was to go on. So we presented the company with a few fowls and investigated the cottage.

It was a startling place. In one bedroom was a lunatic hag with some food by her side. We left her severely alone. Poor soul, we could not move her! In the kitchen we discovered coffee, sugar, salt, and onions. With the aid of our old Post Sergeant we plucked some of the chickens and put on a great stew. I made a huge basin full of coffee.

The others, dead tired, went to sleep in a wee loft. I could not sleep. I was always seeing those wounded men passing, passing, and in my ear—like the maddening refrain of a musical comedy ditty—there was always murmuring—"We shall never return. It doesn't matter." Outside was the clink and clatter of the column, the pitiful curses of tired men, the groaning roar of the motor-lorries as they toiled up the slope.

Then the Staff began to wander in one by one—on foot, exhausted and bedraggled. They loved the coffee, but only played with the chicken—I admit it was tough. They thought all was lost and the General killed. One murmured to another: "Magersfontein, Dour, and this—you've had some successful battles."

And one went to sleep, but kept starting up, and giving a sort of strangled shout—"All gone! All gone!"

When each had rested awhile he would ask gently for a little more coffee, rub his eyes, and disappear into the column to tramp through the night to Saint Quentin. It was the purest melodrama.

And I, too tired to sleep, too excited to think, sat sipping thick coffee the whole night through, while the things that were happening soaked into me like petrol into a rag. About two hours before dawn I pulled myself together and climbed into the loft for forty minutes' broken slumber.

An hour before dawn we wearily dressed. The others devoured cold stew, and immediately there was the faintest glimmering of light we went outside. The column was still passing—such haggard, broken men! The others started off, but for some little time I could not get my engine to fire. Then I got going. Quarter of a mile back I came upon a little detachment of the Worcesters marching in perfect order, with a cheery subaltern at their head. He shouted a greeting in passing. It was Urwick, a friend of mine at Oxford.

I cut across country, running into some of our cavalry on the way. It was just light enough for me to see properly when my engine jibbed. I cleaned a choked petrol pipe, lit a briar—never have I tasted anything so good—and pressed on.

Very bitter I felt, and when nearing Saint Quentin, some

French soldiers got in my way, I cursed them in French, then in German, and finally in good round English oaths for cowards, and I know not what. They looked very startled and recoiled into the ditch. I must have looked alarming—a gaunt, dirty, unshaven figure towering above my motor-cycle, without hat, bespattered with mud, and eyes bright and weary for want of sleep. How I hated the French! I hated them because, as I then thought, they had deserted us at Mons and again at Le Cateau; I hated them because they had the privilege of seeing the British Army in confused retreat; I hated them because their roads were very nearly as bad as the roads of the Belgians. So, wet, miserable, and angry, I came into Saint Quentin just as the sun was beginning to shine a little.

Chapter 5
The Great Retreat

On the morning of the 27th we draggled into Saint Quentin. I found the others gorged with coffee and cakes provided by a kindly Staff-Officer. I imitated them and looked around. Troops of all arms were passing through very wearily. The people stood about, listless and sullen. Everywhere proclamations were posted beseeching the inhabitants to bring in all weapons they might possess. We found the Signal Company, and rode ahead of it out of the town to some fields above a village called Castres. There we unharnessed and took refuge from the gathering storm under a half-demolished haystack. The Germans didn't agree to our remaining for more than fifty minutes. Orders came for us to harness up and move on. I was left behind with the H.Q.S., which had collected itself, and was sent a few minutes later to 2nd Corps H.Q. at Ham, a ride of about fifteen miles.

On the way I stopped at an inn and discovered there three or four of our motor-cyclists, who had cut across country, and an officer. The officer[8] told us how he had been sent on to construct trenches at Le Cateau. It seems that although he enlisted civilian help, he had neither the time nor the men to construct more than very makeshift affairs, which were afterwards but slightly improved by the men who occupied them.

Five minutes and I was on the road again. It was an easy run, something of a joy-ride until, nearing Ham, I ran into a train of

8. I do not know who the officer was, and I give the story as I wrote it in a letter home—for what it is worth.

motor-lorries, which of all the parasites that infest the road are the most difficult to pass. Luckily for me they were travelling in the opposite direction to mine, so I waited until they passed and then rode into Ham and delivered my message.

The streets of Ham were almost blocked by a confused column retreating through it. Officers stationed at every corner and bend were doing their best to reduce it to some sort of order, but with little success.

Returning I was forced into a byroad by the column, lost my way, took the wrong road out of the town, but managed in about a couple of hours to pick up the Signal Co., which by this time had reached the Chateau at Oleezy.

There was little rest for us that night. Twice I had to run into Ham. The road was bad and full of miscellaneous transport. The night was dark, and a thick mist clung to the road. Returning the second time, I was so weary that I jogged on about a couple of miles beyond my turning before I woke up sufficiently to realise where I was.

The next morning (the 28th) we were off before dawn. So tired were we that I remember we simply swore at each other for nothing at all. We waited, shivering in the morning cold, until the column was well on its way.

At Oleezy the Division began to find itself. Look at the map and think for a moment what the men had done. On the 21st they had advanced from Landrecies to Bavai, a fair day's march on a blazing day. On the 22nd they had marched from Bavai to the Canal. From the morning of the 23rd to midday or later on the 24th they had fought hard. On the afternoon and evening of the 24th they had retired to the Bavai-Saint-Waast line. Before dawn on the morning of the 25th they had started off again and marched in column of route on another blazing day back to a position a few miles south of Le Cateau. The battle had begun as the sun rose on the 26th, and continued until three o'clock or later in the afternoon. They plodded through the darkness and the rain. No proper halt was made until midday of the 27th.

The General, who had escaped, and the Staff worked with ferocious energy, as we very painfully knew. Battalions bivouacked in the open fields round Oleezy collected the stragglers that came in and reorganised themselves. The cavalry were between us and Saint Quentin. We were in communication with them by despatch rider. Trains full of French troops passed westwards over Oleezy bridge. There were, I believe, General d'Amade's two reserve divisions. We had walked away from the Germans.

We rode after the column. On the way we passed a battalion of men who had been on outpost duty with nothing but a biscuit and a half apiece. They broke their ranks to snatch at some meat that had been dumped by the roadside, and gnawed it furiously as they marched along until the blood ran down from their chins on to their jackets.

I shall never forget how our General saw a batch of Gordons and K.O.S.B. stragglers trudging listlessly along the road. He halted them. Some more came up until there was about a company in all, and with one piper. He made them form fours, put the piper at the head of them. "Now, lads, follow the piper, and remember Scotland"; and they all started off as pleased as Punch with the tired piper playing like a hero.

Oving or the Fat Boy volunteered to take a message to a body of cavalry that was covering our rear. He found them, and then, being mapless (maps were very scarce in those days), he lost his way. There was no sun, so he rode in what he thought was the right direction, until suddenly he discovered that he was two kilometres from Saint Quentin. As the Germans were officially reported to be five miles south of the town he turned back and fled into the darkness. He slept that night at a cottage, and picked up the Division in the morning.

I was sent on to fill up with petrol wherever I could find it. I was forced to ride on for about four miles to some cross-roads. There I found a staff-car that had some petrol to spare. It was now very hot, so I had a bit of a sleep on the dusty grass by the side of the road, then sat up to watch lazily the 2nd Corps pass.

The troops were quite cheerful and on the whole marching well. There were a large number of stragglers, but the majority of them were not men who had fallen out, but men who had become separated from their battalions at Le Cateau. A good many were badly footsore. These were being crowded into lorries and cars.

There was one solitary desolate figure. He was evidently a reservist, a feeble little man of about forty, with three days' growth on his chin. He was very, very tired, but was struggling along with an unconquerable spirit. I gave him a little bit of chocolate I had; but he wouldn't stop to eat it. "I can't stop. If I does, I shall never get there." So he chewed it, half-choking, as he stumbled along. I went a few paces after him. Then Captain Dillon came up, stopped us, and put the poor fellow in a staff-car and sent him along a few miles in solitary grandeur, more nervous than comfortable.

Eventually the company came along and I joined. Two miles farther we came to a biggish town with white houses that simply glared with heat.[9] My water-bottle was empty, so I humbly approached a good lady who was doling out cider and water at her cottage door. It did taste good! A little farther on I gave up my bicycle to Spuggy, who was riding in the cable-cart.

We jolted along at about two miles an hour. For some time two spies under escort walked beside the limber. Unlike most spies they looked their part. One was tall and thin and handsome. The other was short and fat and ugly. The fear of death was on their faces, and the jeers of our men died in their mouths. They were marched along for two days until a Court could be convened. Then they were shot.

Just before Noyon we turned off to the left and halted for half an hour at Landrimont, a little village full of big trees. We had omelettes and coffee at the inn, then basked in the sun and smoked. Noyon was unattractive. The people did not seem to care what happened to anybody. Perhaps we thought that, because we were very tired. Outside Noyon I dozed, then went off to sleep.

When I awoke it was quite dark, and the column had halted. The order came for all except the drivers to dismount and proceed on foot. The bridge ahead was considered unsafe, so wagons went across singly.

---

9. It must have been Guiscard.

I walked on into the village, Pontoise. There were no lights, and the main street was illuminated only by the lanterns of officers seeking their billets. An A.S.C. officer gave me a lift. Our H.Q. were right the other end of the town in the Chateau of the wee hamlet called La Pommeraye. I found them, stumbled into a loft, and dropped down for a sleep.

We were called fairly late.[10] George and I rode into Pontoise and "scrounged" for eggs and bread. These we took to a small and smelly cottage. The old woman of the cottage boiled our eggs and gave us coffee. It was a luxurious breakfast. I was looking forward to a slack lazy day in the sun, for we were told that we had for the moment outdistanced the gentle Germans. But my turn came round horribly soon, and I was sent off to Compiègne with a message for G.H.Q., and orders to find our particularly elusive Div. Train. It was a gorgeous ride along a magnificent road, through the great forest, and I did the twenty odd miles in forty odd minutes.

G.H.Q. was installed in the Palace. Everybody seemed very clean and lordly, and for a moment I was ashamed of my dirty, ragged, unshorn self. Then I realised that I was "from the Front"—a magic phrase to conjure with for those behind the line—and swaggered through long corridors.

After delivering my message I went searching for the Div. Train. First, I looked round the town for it, then I had wind of it at the station, but at the station it had departed an hour or so before. I returned to G.H.Q., but there they knew nothing. I tried every road leading out of the town. Finally, having no map, and consequently being unable to make a really thorough search, I had a drink, and started off back.

When I returned I found everybody was getting ready to move, so I packed up. This time the motor-cyclists rode in advance of the column. About two miles out I found that the others had dropped behind out of sight. I went on into Carlepont, and made myself useful to the Billeting Officer. The others arrived later. It seems there had been a rumour of Uhlans on the road, and they had come along fearfully.

10. August 29th.

The troops marched in, singing and cheering. It was unbelievable what half a day's rest had done for them. Of course you must remember that we all firmly believed, except in our moments of deepest despondency, first, that we could have held the Germans at Mons and Le Cateau if the French had not "deserted" us, and second, that our retreat was merely a *"mouvement stratégique."*

There was nothing doing at the Signal Office, so we went and had some food—cold sausage and coffee. Our hostess was buxom and hilarious. There was also a young girl about the place, Hélène. She was of a middle size, serious and dark, with a mass of black lustreless hair. She could not have been more than nineteen. Her baby was put to bed immediately we arrived. We loved them both, because they were the first women we had met since Mons who had not wanted to know why we were retreating and had not received the same answer—*"mouvement stratégique pour attaquer le mieux."* I had a long talk that night with Hélène as she stood at her door. Behind us the dark square was filled with dark sleeping soldiers, the noise of snoring and the occasional clatter of moving horses. Finally, I left her and went to sleep on the dusty boards of an attic in the Chateau.

We were called when it was still dark and very cold (August 30). I was vainly trying to warm myself at a feeble camp fire when the order came to move off—without breakfast. The dawn was just breaking when we set out—to halt a hundred yards or so along. There we shivered for half an hour with nothing but a pipe and a scrap of chocolate that had got stuck at the bottom of my greatcoat pocket. Finally, the motor-cyclists, to their great relief, were told that they might go on ahead. The Grimers and I cut across a country to get away from the column. We climbed an immense hill in the mist, and proceeding by a devious route eventually bustled into Attichy, where we found a large and dirty inn containing nothing but some bread and jam. The column was scheduled to go ten miles farther, but "the situation being favourable" it was decided to go no farther. Headquarters were established by the roadside, and I was sent off to a jolly village right up on the hill to halt some sappers, and then back along the column to give the various units the names of their billets.

We supped off the sizzling bacon and slept on the grass by the side of the road. That night George burned his Rudge. It was an accident, but we were none too sorry, for it had given much trouble. There were messages right through the night. At one in the morning I was sent off to a Chateau in the Forest of Compiègne. I had no map, and it was a pure accident that I found my way there and back.

The next day (Aug. 31) was a joyous ride. We went up and down hills to a calm, lazy little village, Haute Fontaine. There we took a wrong turning and found ourselves in a blackberry lane. It was the hottest, pleasantest of days, and forgetting all about the more serious things—we could not even hear the guns—we filled up with the softest, ripest of fruit. Three of us rode together, N'Soon, Grimers, and myself. I don't know how we found our way. We just wandered on through sleepy, cobbled villages, along the top of ridges with great misty views and by quiet streams. Just beyond a village stuck on to the side of a hill, we came to a river, and through the willows we saw a little church. It was just like the Happy Valley that's over the fields from Burford.

We all sang anything we could remember as we rattled along. The bits of columns that we passed did not damp us, for they consisted only of transport, and transport can never be tragic—even in a retreat. The most it can do is to depress you with a sense of unceasing monotonous effort.

About three o'clock we came to a few houses—Béthancourt. There was an omelette, coffee, and pears for us at the inn. The people were frightened.

Why are the English retreating? Are they defeated?

No, it is only a strategical movement.

Will the dirty Germans pass by here? We had better pack up our traps and fly.

We were silent for a moment, then I am afraid I lied blandly.

Oh no, this is as far as we go.

But I had reckoned without my host, a lean, wiry old fellow, a bit stiff about the knees. First of all he proudly showed me his soldier's book—three campaigns in Algeria. A crowd of smelly women pressed round us—luckily we had finished our meal—

while with the help of a few knives and plates he explained exactly what a strategical movement was, and demonstrated to the satisfaction of everybody except ourselves that the valley we were in was obviously the place *"pour reculer le mieux."*

We had been told that our H.O. was going to be at a place called Béthisy St Martin, so on we went. A couple of miles from Béthisy we came upon a billeting party of officers sitting in the shade of a big tree by the side of the road. Had we heard that the Germans were at Compiègne, ten miles or so over the hill? No, we hadn't. Was it safe to go on into Béthisy? None of us had an idea. We stopped and questioned a "civvy" push-cyclist. He had just come from Béthisy and had seen no Germans. The officers started arguing whether or no they should wait for an escort. We got impatient and slipped on. Of course there was nothing in Béthisy except a wide-eyed population, a selection of smells, and a vast congregation of chickens. The other two basked on some hay in the sun, while I went back and pleased myself immensely by reporting to the officers who were timorously trotting along that there wasn't a sign of a Uhlan.

We rested a bit. One of us suggested having a look round for some Uhlans from the top of the nearest hill. It was a terrific climb up a narrow track, but our bicycles brought us up magnificently. From the top we could see right away to the forest of Compiègne, but a judicious bit of scouting produced nothing.

Coming down we heard from a passing car that H.Q. were to be at Crêpy-en-Valois, a biggish old place about four miles away to the south the other side of Béthancourt. We arrived there just as the sun was going to set. It was a confusing place, crammed full of transport, but I found my way to our potential H.Q. with the aid of a joyous little flapper on my carrier.

Then I remembered I had left my revolver behind on the hill above Béthisy. Just before I started I heard that there were bags of Uhlans coming along over the hills and through the woods. But there was nothing for it but to go back, and back I went. It was a bestial climb in the dusk. On my way back I saw some strange-looking figures in the grounds of a chateau. So I opened my throttle and thundered past.

Later I found that the figures belonged to the rest of the motor-cyclists. The chateau ought to have been our H.Q., and arriving there they had been entertained to a sit-down tea and a bath.

We had a rotten night—nothing between me and a cold, hard tiled floor except a waterproof sheet, but no messages.

We woke very early (September 1st) to the noise of guns. The Germans were attacking vigorously, having brought up several brigades of Jaegers by motor-bus. The 15th was on our left, the 13th was holding the hill above Béthancourt, and the 14th was scrapping away on the right. The guns were ours, as the Germans didn't appear to have any with them. I did a couple of messages out to the 15th. The second time I came back with the news that their left flank was being turned.

A little later one of our despatch riders rode in hurriedly. He reported that, while he was riding along the road to the 15th, he had been shot at by Uhlans whom he had seen distinctly. At the moment it was of the utmost importance to get a despatch through to the 15th. The Skipper offered to take it, but the General refused his offer.

A second despatch rider was carefully studying his map. It seemed to him absolutely inconceivable that Uhlans should be at the place where the first despatch rider had seen them. They must either have ridden right round our left flank and left rear, or else broken through the line. So he offered boldly to take the despatch.

He rode by a slightly roundabout road, and reached the 15th in safety. On his way back he saw a troop of North Irish Horse. In the meantime the Divisional Headquarters had left Crépy in great state, the men with rifles in front, and taken refuge on a hill south-east of the town. On his return the despatch rider was praised mightily for his work, but to this day he believes the Uhlans were North Irish Horse and the bullets "overs"[11]—to this day the first despatch rider contradicts him.

The Division got away from Crépy with the greatest success. The 13th slaughtered those foolish Huns that tried to charge up the hill in the face of rifle, machine-gun, and a considerable shell

11. Stray bullets that, fired too high, miss their mark, and occasionally hit men well behind the actual firing line.

fire. The Duke of Wellington's laid a pretty little ambush and hooked a car containing the general and staff of the 1st Cavalry Division. The prisoners were remorsefully shot, as it would have been impossible to bring them away under the heavy fire.

We jogged on to Nanteuil, all of us very pleased with ourselves, particularly the Duke of Wellington's, who were loaded with spoils, and a billeting officer who, running slap into some Uhlans, had been fired at all the way from 50 yards' range to 600 and hadn't been hit.

I obtained leave to give a straggler a lift of a couple of miles. He was embarrassingly grateful. The last few miles was weary work for the men. Remember they had marched or fought, or more often both, every day since our quiet night at Landrecies. The road, too, was the very roughest *pavé*, though I remember well a little forest of bracken and pines we went through. Being "a would-be literary bloke," I murmured "Scottish"; being tired I forgot it from the moment after I saw it until now.

There was no rest at Nanteuil. I took the Artillery Staff Captain round the brigades on my carrier, and did not get back until 10. A bit of hot stew and a post-card from home cheered me. I managed a couple of hours' sleep.

We turned out about 3, the morning of September 2nd. It was quite dark and bitterly cold. Very sleepily indeed we rode along an exiguous path by the side of the cobbles. The sun had risen, but it was still cold when we rattled into that diabolical city of lost souls, Dammartin.

Nobody spoke as we entered. Indeed there were only a few haggard, ugly old women, each with a bit of a beard and a large goitre. One came up to me and chattered at me. Then suddenly she stopped and rushed away, still gibbering. We asked for a restaurant. A stark, silent old man, with a goitre, pointed out an *estaminet*. There we found four motionless men, who looked up at us with expressionless eyes. Chilled, we withdrew into the street. Silent, melancholy soldiers—the H.Q. of some army or division—were marching miserably out. We battered at the door of a hotel for twenty minutes. We stamped and cursed and swore, but no one would open. Only a hideous and filthy crowd stood round, and not one of them moved a muscle. Finally, we burst into a bare little inn, and had such a desolate breakfast of sour wine, bread, and bully. We finished as soon as we could to leave the nightmare place. Even the houses were gaunt and ill-favoured.

On our way out we came across a deserted motor-cycle. Some one suggested sending it on by train, until some one else remarked that there were no trains, and this was fifteen miles from Paris.

We cut across country, rejoined the column, and rode with it to Vinantes, passing on the way a lost motor-lorry. The driver was tearing his hair in an absolute panic. We told him the Germans were just a few miles along the road; but we wished we hadn't when, in hurriedly reversing to escape, he sent a couple of us into the ditch.

At Vinantes we "requisitioned" a car, some chickens, and a pair of boots. There was a fusty little tavern down the street, full of laughing soldiers. In the corner a fat, middle-aged woman sat weeping quietly on a sack. The host, sullen and phlegmatic, answered every question with a shake of the head and a muttered *"N'importe."* The money he threw contemptuously on the counter. The soldiers thought they were spies. "As speaking the langwidge," I asked him what the matter was.

"They say, sir, that this village will be shelled by the cursed Germans, and the order has gone out to evacuate."

Then, suddenly his face became animated, and he told me volubly how he had been born in the village, how he had been married there, how he had kept the *estaminet* for twenty years, how all the leading men of the village came of an evening and talked over the things that were happening in Paris.

He started shouting, as men will—

"What does it matter what I sell, what I receive? What does it matter, for have I not to leave all this?"

Then his wife came up and put her hand on his arm—

"Now, now; give the gentlemen their beer."

I bought some cherry brandy and came away.

I was sent on a couple of messages that afternoon: one to trace a telephone wire to a deserted station with nothing in it but a sack of excellent potatoes, another to an officer whom

I could not find. I waited under a tree eating somebody else's pears until I was told he had gone mad, and was wandering aimlessly about.

It was a famous night for me. I was sent off to Dammartin, and knew something would go wrong. It did. A sentry all but shot me. I nearly rode into an unguarded trench across the road, and when I started back with my receipt my bicycle would not fire. I found that the mechanic at Dammartin had filled my tank with water. It took me two hours, two lurid hours, to take that water out. It was three in the morning when I got going. I was badly frightened the Division had gone on, because I hadn't the remotest conception where it was going to. When I got back H.Q. were still at Vinantes. I retired thankfully to my bed under the stars, listening dreamily to Grimers, who related how a sentry had fired at him, and how one bullet had singed the back of his neck.

We left Vinantes not too early after breakfast—a comfort, as we had all of us been up pretty well the whole night. Grimers was still upset at having been shot at by sentries. I had been going hard, and had had only a couple of hours' sleep. We rode on in advance of the company. It was very hot and dusty, and when we arrived at Crécy with several hours to spare, we first had a most excellent omelette and then a shave, a hair-cut, and a wash. Crécy was populous and excited. It made us joyous to think we had reached a part of the country where the shops were open, people pursuing their own business, where there was no dumbly reproaching glance for us in our retreat.

We had been told that our H.Q. that night were going to be at the chateau of a little village called La Haute Maison. Three of us arrived there and found the caretaker just leaving. We obtained the key, and when he had gone did a little bit of looting on our own. First we had a great meal of lunch-tongue, bread, wine, and stewed pears. Then we carefully took half a dozen bottles of champagne and hid them, together with some other food-stuffs, in the middle of a big bed of nettles. A miscellaneous crowd of cows were wandering round the house lowing pitifully.

We were just about to make a heroic effort at milking when the 3rd Div. billeting officer arrived and told us that the 5th Div.

H.Q. would be that night at Bouleurs, farther back. We managed to carry off the food-stuffs, but the champagne is probably still in the nettles. And the bottles are standing up too.

We found the company encamped in a schoolhouse, our fat signal-sergeant doing dominie at the desk. I made himself a comfortable sleeping-place with straw, then went out on the road to watch the refugees pass.

I don't know what it was. It may have been the bright and clear evening glow, but—you will laugh—the refugees seemed to me absurdly beautiful. A dolorous, patriarchal procession of old men with white beards leading their asthmatic horses that drew huge country carts piled with clothes, furniture, food, and pets. Frightened cows with heavy swinging udders were being piloted by lithe middle-aged women. There was one girl demurely leading goats. In the full crudity of curve and distinctness of line she might have sat for Steinlen—there was a brownness, too, in the atmosphere. Her face was olive and of perfect proportions; her eyelashes long and black. She gave me a terrified side-glance, and I thought I was looking at the picture of the village flirt in serene flight.

I connect that girl with a whisky-and-soda, drunk about midnight out of a tin mug under the trees, thanks to the kindness of the Divisional Train officers. It did taste fine.

The next day (September 4th) I was attached to the Divisional Cyclists. We spent several hours on the top of a hill, looking right across the valley for Germans. I was glad of the rest, as very early in the morning I had been sent off at full speed to prevent an officer blowing up a bridge. Luckily I blundered into one of his men, and scooting across a mile of heavy plough, I arrived breathless at the bridge, but just in time. The bridge in the moonlight looked like a patient horse waiting to be whipped on the raw. The subaltern was very angry. There had been an alarm of Uhlans, and his French escort had retired from the bridge to safer quarters....

I shared Captain Burnett's lunch, and later went to fetch some men from a bridge that we had blown up. It seemed to me at the time that the bridge had been blown up very badly. As a matter of fact, German infantry crossed it four hours after I had left it.

We had "the wind up" that afternoon. It appears that a patrol of six Uhlans had either been cut off or had somehow got across the river at Meaux. Anyway, they rode past an unsuspecting sleepy outpost of ours, and spread alarm through the division. Either the division was panicky or the report had become exaggerated on the way to H.Q. Batteries were put into position on the Meaux road, and there was a general liveliness.

I got back from a hard but unexciting day's work with the Cyclists to find that the Germans had got across in very fact, though not at Meaux, and that we were going to do a further bunk that night. We cursed the gentle Germans heartily and well. About 10.30 the three of us who were going on started. We found some convoys on the way, delivered messages, and then I, who was leading, got badly lost in the big Villeneuve forest—I forgot the name of it at the moment.[12] Of course I pretended that we were taking the shortest road, and luck, which is always with me when I've got to find anything, didn't desert me that night.

At dead of night we echoed into the Chateau at Tournan, roused some servants, and made them get us some bread, fruit, and mattresses. The bread and fruit we devoured, together with a lunch-tongue, from that excellent Chateau at La Haute Maison—the mattresses we took into a large airy room and slept on, until we were wakened by the peevish tones of the other motor-cyclists who had ridden with the column. One of them had fallen asleep on his bicycle and disappeared into a ditch, but the other two were so sleepy they did not hear him. We were all weary and bad-tempered, while a hot dusty day, and a rapid succession of little routine messages, did not greatly cheer us.

At Tournan, appropriately, we turned. We were only a few miles S.-E. of Paris. The Germans never got farther than Lagny. There they came into touch with our outposts, so the tactful French are going to raise a monument to Jeanne d'Arc—a reminder, I suppose, that even we and they committed atrocities sometime.

---

12. Forêt de Crécy.

CHAPTER 6

Over the Marne to the Aisne

The morning of September 5th was very hot, but the brigades could easily be found, and the roads to them were good. There was cheerfulness in the air. A rumour went round—it was quite incredible, and we scoffed—that instead of further retreating either beyond or into the fortifications of Paris, there was a possibility of an advance. The Germans, we were told, had at last been outflanked. Joffre's vaunted plan that had inspired us through the dolorous startled days of retirement was, it appeared, a fact, and not one of those bright fancies that the Staff invents for our tactical delectation.

Spuggy returned. He had left us at Bouleurs to find a bicycle in Paris. Coming back he had no idea that we had moved. So he rode too far north. He escaped luckily. He was riding along about three hundred yards behind two motor-cyclists. Suddenly he saw them stop abruptly and put up their hands. He fled. A little farther on he came to a village and asked for coffee. He heard that Uhlans had been there a few hours before, and was taken to see a woman who had been shot through the breast. Then he went south through Villeneuve, and following a fortunate instinct, ran into our outposts the other side of Tournan.

We all slept grandly on mattresses. It was the first time we had been two nights in the same place since Dour.

We awoke early to a gorgeous day. We were actually going to advance. The news put us in marvellous good temper. For the first time in my recollection we offered each other our bacon, and one at the end of breakfast said he had had enough. The

Staff was almost giggling, and a battalion (the Cheshires, I think) that we saw pass, was absolutely shouting with joy. You would have thought we had just gained a famous victory.

Half of us went forward with the column. The rest remained for a slaughterous hour. First we went to the hen-house, and in ten minutes had placed ten dripping victims in the French gendarme captain's car. Then George and I went in pursuit of a turkey for the Skipper. It was an elusive bird with a perfectly Poultonian swerve, but with a bagful of curses, a bleeding hand, and a large stick, I did it to death.

We set out merrily and picked up Spuggy, Cecil, and George in the big forest that stretches practically from the Marne to Tournan. They thought they had heard a Uhlan, but nothing came of it (he turned out to be a deer), so we went on to Villeneuve. There I bought some biscuits and George scrounged some butter. A job to the 3rd Division on our right and another in pursuit of an errant officer, and then a sweaty and exiguous lunch—it was a sweltering noon—seated on a blistering pavement. Soon after lunch three of us were sent on to Mortcerf, a village on a hill to the north of the forest. We were the first English there—the Germans had left it in the morning—and the whole population, including one strikingly pretty flapper, turned out to welcome us in their best clean clothes—it may have been Sunday.

We accepted any quantity of gorgeous, luscious fruit, retiring modestly to a shady log to eat it, and smoke a delectable pipe. In a quarter of an hour Major Hildebrand of the 2nd Corps turned up in his car, and later the company.

Pollers had had a little adventure. He was with some of our men when he saw a grey figure coming down one of the glades to the road. We knew there were many stray Uhlans in the forest who had been left behind by our advance. The grey figure was stalked, unconscious of his danger. Pollers had a shot with his revolver, luckily without effect, for the figure turned out to be our blasphemous farrier, who had gone into the forest, clad only in regulation grey shirt and trousers, to find some water.

Later in the afternoon I was sent off to find the North Irish

Horse. I discovered them four miles away in the first flush of victory. They had had a bit of a scrap with Uhlans, and were proudly displaying to an admiring brigade that was marching past a small but select collection of horses, lances, and saddles.

This afternoon George smashed up his bicycle, the steering head giving at a corner.

We bivouacked on the drive, but the hardness of our bed didn't matter, as we were out all night—all of us, including the two, Grimers and Cecil. It was nervous riding in the forest. All the roads looked exactly alike, and down every glade we expected a shot from derelict Uhlans. That night I thought out plots for at least four stories. It would have been three, but I lost my way, and was only put right by striking a wandering convoy. I was in search of the Division Train. I looked for it at Tournan and at Villeneuve and right through the forest, but couldn't find it. I was out from ten to two, and then again from two to five, with messages for miscellaneous ammunition columns. I collared an hour's sleep and, by mistake, a chauffeur's overcoat, which led to recriminations in the morning. But the chauffeur had an unfair advantage. I was too tired to reply.

Grimers, who cannot see well at night, was terrified when he had to take a despatch through the forest. He rode with a loaded revolver in one hand, and was only saved from shooting a wretched transport officer by a wild cry, "For God's sake, look what you're doing."

The eldest Cecil reported a distinct smell of dead horses at the obelisk in the forest. At least he rather thought they were dead donkeys. The smell was a little different—more acrid and unpleasant. We told him that there were eight dead Germans piled at the side of the road, and we reminded him that it had been a sweltering day.

We were terribly tired in the morning. Spuggy, George, and Orr went off to Paris for new bicycles, and we were left short-handed again. Another tropical day.

The Skipper rode the spare bike with great dash, the elder Cecil and I attendant. We sprinted along a good straight road to the cobbled, crowded little town of Faremoutiers. Then we decided to advance to Mouroux, our proposed headquarters. It was a haggard village, just off the road. We arrived there about twelve: the Germans had departed at six, leaving behind them a souvenir in the dead body of a fellow from the East Lancs. crumpled in a ditch. He had been shot while eating. It was my first corpse. I am afraid I was not overwhelmed with thoughts of the fleetingness of life or the horror of death. If I remember my feelings aright, they consisted of a pinch of sympathy mixed with a trifle of disgust, and a very considerable hunger, which some apples by the roadside did something to allay.

I shall never forget Mouroux. It was just a little square of old houses. Before the Mairie was placed a collection of bottles from which the Sales Boches had very properly drunk. French proclamations were scribbled over with coarse, heavy jests. The women were almost hysterical with relieved anxiety. The men were still sullen, and, though they looked well fed, begged for bread. A German knapsack that I had picked up and left in charge of some villagers was torn to shreds in fierce hatred when my back was turned.

It was very lonely there in the sun. We had outstripped the advance-guard by mistake and were relieved when it came up.

We made prisoner of a German who had overslept himself because he had had a bath.

I rushed back with Grimers on my carrier to fetch another bicycle. On my return my engine suddenly produced an unearthly metallic noise. It was only an aeroplane coming down just over my head.

In the late afternoon we marched into Coulommiers. The people crowded into the streets and cheered us. The girls, with tears in their eyes, handed us flowers.

Three of us went to the Mairie. The Maire, a courtly little fellow in top-hat and frock-coat, welcomed us in charming terms. Two fat old women rushed up to us and besought us to allow them to do something for us. We set one to make us tea, and the other to bring us hot water and soap.

A small girl of about eight brought me her kitten and wanted to give it me. I explained to her that it would not be very comfortable tied with pink ribbons to my carrier. She gravely assented, sat on my knee, told me I was very dirty, and commanded me to kill heaps and heaps of Germans. She didn't like them; they had beards!

You know those fierce middle-aged Frenchwomen of the *bourgeois* class, hard as Scotsmen, close as Jews, and with feelings about as fine as those of a motor-bus. She was one of them, and she was the foremost of a largish crowd that collected round me. With her was a pretty girl of about twenty-two.

The mother began with a rhetorical outburst against all Germans, anathematising in particular those who had spent the last fortnight in Coulommiers, in which town her uncle had set up his business, which, though it had proved successful, as they all knew, &c., &c. The crowd murmured that they did all know. Then the old harridan chanted the wrongs which the Germans had wrought until, when she had worked the crowd and herself up to a heat of furious excitement, she lowered her voice, suddenly lowered her tone. In a grating whisper she narrated, in more detail than I cared to hear, the full story of how her daughter—to whom she pointed—had been shamefully treated by the Germans. The crowd growled. The daughter was, I think, more pleased at being the object of my sympathy and the centre of the crowd's interest than agonised at the remembrance of her misfortune.

Some of the company coming up saved me from the recital of further outrages. The hag told them of a house where the Germans had left a rifle or two and some of our messages which they had intercepted. The girl hesitated a moment, and then followed. I started hastily to go on, but the girl, hearing the noise of my engine, ran back to bid me an unembarrassed farewell.

I rode through Coulommiers, a jolly rambling old town, to our billet in a suburban villa on the Rebais road. The Division was marching past in the very best of spirits. We, who were very tired, endeavoured to make ourselves comfortable—we were then blanketless—on the abhorrent surface of a narrow garden path.

That night a 2nd Corps despatch rider called in half an hour before his death. We have heard many explanations of how he died. He crashed into a German barricade, and we discovered him the next morning with his eyes closed, neatly covered with a sheet, in a quaint little house at the entrance to the village of Doué.

At dawn (Sept. 8th) the others went on with the column. I was sent back with a despatch for Faremoutiers, and then was detailed to remain for an hour with Cecil. Ten minutes after my return the Fat Boy rode in, greatly excited. He had gone out along the Aulnoy road with a message, and round a corner had run into a patrol of Uhlans. He kept his head, turned quickly, and rode off in a shower of bullets. He was tremendously indignant, and besought some cavalry who were passing to go in pursuit.

We heard the rumble of guns and started in a hurry after the column. Sergeant Merchant's bicycle—our spare, a Rudge—burnt out its clutch, and we left it in exchange for some pears at a cottage with a delicious garden in Champbreton. Doué was a couple of miles farther on.

Colonel Sawyer, D.D.M.S., stopped me anxiously, and asked me to go and see if I could recognise the despatch rider's corpse. I meditated over it for a few minutes, then ran on to the signal-office by the roadside. There I exchanged my old bike for a new one which had been discovered in a cottage. Nothing was wrong with my ancient grid except a buckled back rim, due to collision with a brick when riding without a lamp. One of the company rode it quietly to Serches, then it went on the side-car, and was eventually discarded at Beuvry.

I found the Division very much in action. The object of the Germans was, by an obstinate rearguard action, to hold first the line of the Petit Morin and second the line La Ferté to the hills north of Méry, so that their main body might get back across the Marne and continue northward their retreat, necessitated by our pressure on their flank. This retreat again was to be as slow as possible, to prevent an outflanking of the whole.

Our object was obviously to prevent them achieving theirs.

Look at the map and grasp these three things—

1. The two rivers—the Petit Morin debouching so as to cover the German left centre.

2. From La Ferté westwards the rivers run in deep ravines, hemmed in by precipitous thickly-wooded hills.

3. Only two bridges across the Marne remained—one large one at La Ferté and one small one at Saacy.

When I arrived at Doué the Germans were holding the Forest of Jouarre in force. They were in moderate force on the south bank of the Petit Morin, and had some guns, but not many, on the north bank.

Here is a tale of how glory may be forced upon the unwilling.

There were troops on the road running south from Jouarre. They might be Germans retreating. They might be the 3rd Corps advancing. The Staff wanted to know at once, and, although a despatch rider had already been sent west to ride up the road from the south, it was thought that another despatch rider skirting the east side of the Bois de Jouarre might find out more quickly. So the captain called for volunteers.

Now one despatch rider had no stomach for the job. He sat behind a tree and tried to look as if he had not heard the captain's appeal. The sergeant in charge had faith in him and, looking round, said in a loud voice, "Here is Jones!" (it is obviously impolitic for me to give even his nickname, if I wish to tell the truth). The despatch rider jumped up, pretended he knew nothing of what was going forward, and asked what was required. He was told, and with sinking heart enthusiastically volunteered for the job.

He rode off, taking the road by La Chevrie Farm. Beyond the farm the Germans sniped him unmercifully, but (so he told me) he got well down on the tank and rode "all out" until he came to the firing line just south-west of the farm to the north of Chevrie. Major Buckle came out of his ditch to see what was wanted. The rifle fire seemed to increase. The air was buzzing, and just in front of his bicycle multitudinous little spurts of dust flecked the road.

It was distinctly unpleasant, and, as Major Buckle persisted in standing in the middle of the road instead of taking the despatch rider with him into his ditch, the despatch rider had to stand there too, horribly frightened. The Major said it was

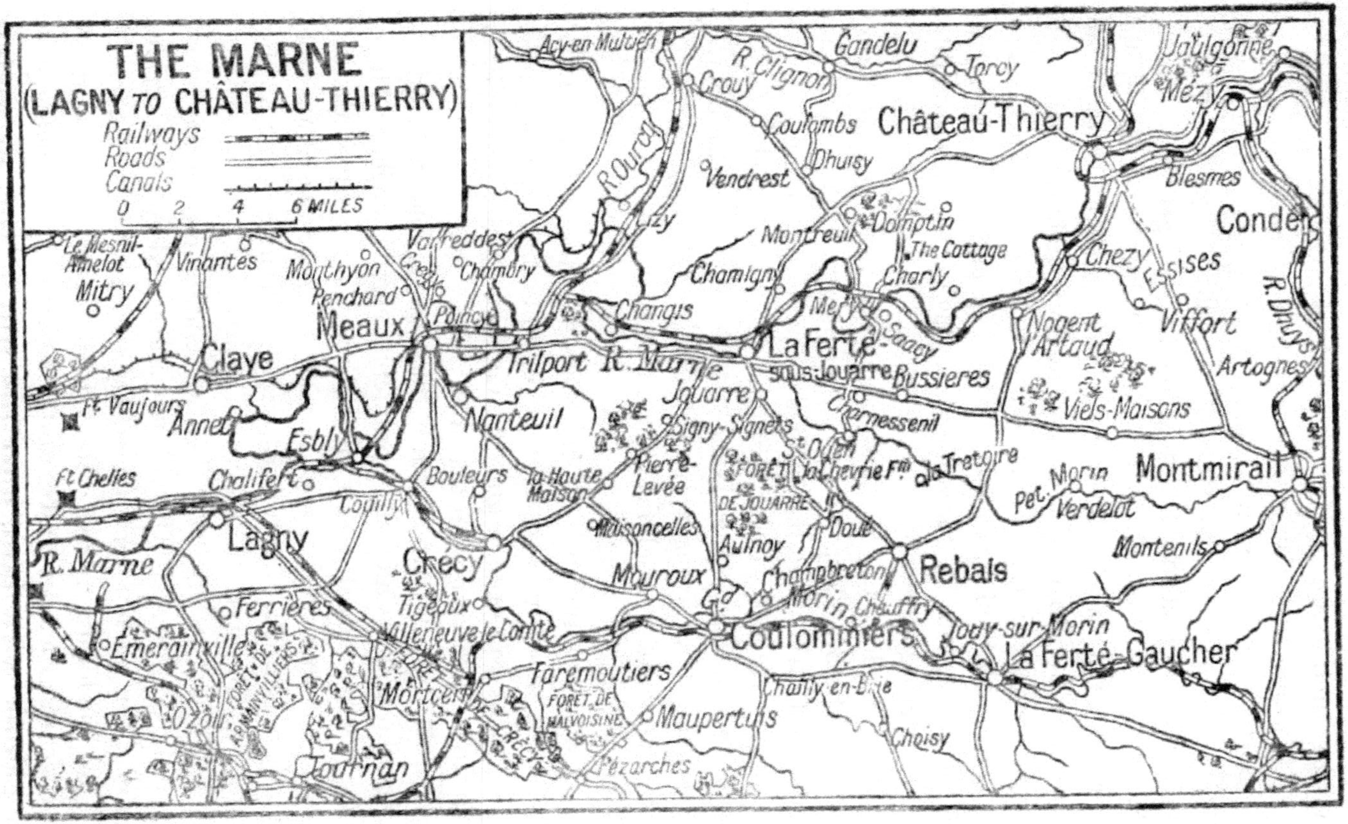
THE MARNE
(LAGNY TO CHÂTEAU-THIERRY)
Railways
Roads
Canals
0 2 4 6 MILES
Acy-en-Multien
Gandelu
Torcy
Jaulgonne
Mézy
R. Clignon
Crouy
Coulombs
Château-Thierry
R. Ourcq
Dhuisy
Vendrest
Blesmes
Condé
Lizy
Montreuil
Domptin
The Cottage
Charly
Chezy
Essises
Viffort
R. Dhuys
Le Mesnil-Amelot
Vinantes
Monthyon
Varreddes
Chambry
Changis
Chamigny
Mitry
Penchard
Meaux
Poincy
Méry
Saacy
Nogent l'Artaud
Claye
Trilport
R. Marne
La Ferté-sous-Jouarre
Bussières
Artognes
Jouarre
Viels-Maisons
Ft. Vaujours
Annet
Nanteuil
Signy-Signets
Charnesseuil
Esbly
St. Ouen
La Trétoire
Montmirail
Ft. Chelles
Chalifert
Bouleurs
La Haute Maison
Pierre-Levée
Forêt de Jouarre
La Chevrie Fm.
Pet. Morin
Verdelot
Couilly
Maisoncelles
Doue
Lagny
Aulnoy
Rebais
Montenils
R. Marne
Crécy
Mouroux
Champbreton
Tigeaux
Morin
Chauffry
Ferrières
Villeneuve le Comte
Coulommiers
Jouy-sur-Morin
Emerainville
La Ferté-Gaucher
Faremoutiers
Mortcerf
Ozoir
Forêt de Malvoisine
Chailly-en-Brie
Maupertuis
Choisy
Tournan
Pézarches

impossible to go farther. There was only a troop of cavalry, taking careful cover, at the farm in front, and—

"My God, man, you're under machine-gun fire."

So that's what it is, murmured the despatch rider to himself, not greatly cheered. He saw he could not get to any vantage point by that road, and it seemed best to get back at once. He absolutely streaked along back to D.H.Q., stopping on the way very much against his will to deliver a message from Major Buckle to the Duke of Wellington's who were in support.

He gave in his report, such as it was, to Colonel Romer, and was praised. Moral: Be called away by some pressing engagement *before* the captain calls for volunteers. May *Gott strafe* thoroughly all interfering sergeants!

The Headquarters Staff advanced in an hour or so to some houses. The 3rd Corps, consisting of the 4th Division and the unlucky 19th Brigade, had pushed on with tremendous dash towards Jouarre, and we learnt from an aeroplane which dropped a message on the hill at Doué that the general situation was favourable. The Germans were crowding across the bridge at La Ferté under heavy shell fire, but unluckily we could not hit the blighted bridge.

It was now midday and very hot. There was little water. We had been advancing over open fields without a vestige of shade.

Under cover of their guns the Germans fled across the Petit Morin in such confusion that they did not even hold the very defensible heights to the north of the river. We followed on their heels through St Ouen and up the hill behind the village. Three of us went on ahead and sat for two hours in a trench with borrowed rifles waiting for the Germans to come out of a wood. But it began to rain very hard, and the Germans came on the other side and were taken by the Cyclists.

It was just getting dark when we rendezvoused at the crossroads of Charnesseuil. The village was battered by our guns, but the villagers did not mind a scrap and welcomed us with screams of joy. The local inn was re-opened with cheers, and in spite of the fact that there were two dead horses, very evil-smelling, just outside, we had drinks all round.

We were interrupted by laughter and cheers. We rushed out to see the quaintest procession coming from the west into Charnesseuil. Seventy odd immense Prussian Guards were humbly pushing in the bicycles of forty of our Divisional Cyclists, who were dancing round them in delight. They had captured a hundred and fifty of them, but our guns had shelled them, luckily without doing much damage to the Cyclists, so loading up the prisoners with all their kit and equipment, and making them lead their captors' bicycles, the Cyclists brought them in triumph for the inspection of the Staff. It was a great moment.

I was very tired, and, careless of who passed, stretched myself at the side of the road for a sleep. I was wakened an hour later, and we all went along together to the chateau. There we slept in the hall before the contented faces of some fine French pictures—or the majority of them—the rest were bestially slashed.

At the break of dawn (Sept. 9th) I was sent off to the 14th Brigade, which composed the advance-guard. Scouts had reported that Saacy had been evacuated by the enemy. So we pushed on cautiously and took possession of the bridge.

I came up with the Brigade Staff on a common at the top of the succeeding hill, having been delayed by a puncture. Nixon, the S.O., told me that a battery of ours in position on the common to the south of the farm would open fire in a few minutes. The German guns would reply, but would be quickly silenced. In the meantime I was to take shelter in the farm.

I had barely put my bicycle under cover in the courtyard when the Germans opened fire, not at our guns but at a couple of companies of the Manchesters who were endeavouring to take cover just north of the farm.

In the farm I found King and his platoon of Cyclists. Shrapnel bullets simply rattled against the old house, and an occasional common shell dropped near by way of variety. The Cyclists were restive, and I was too, so to relieve the situation I proposed breakfast. King and I had half a loaf of Saacy bread and half a pot of jam I always carried about with me. The rest went to the men. Our breakfast was nearly spoilt by the Manchesters, who, after they had lost a few men, rushed through the farm into the wood, where, naturally enough, they lost a few more. They besought the Cyclists to cover their retreat, but as it was from shrapnel we mildly suggested it was impossible.

The courtyard was by this time covered with tiles and pitted with bullets. We, close up against the wall, had been quite moderately safe. The shelling slackened off, so we thought we had better do a bunk. With pride of race the motor-cyclist left last.

The 14th Brigade had disappeared. I went back down the track and found the General and his staff, fuming, half-way up the hill. The German guns could not be found, and the German guns were holding up the whole Division.

I slept by the roadside for an hour. I was woken up to take a message to 2nd Corps at Saacy. On my return I was lucky enough to see a very spectacular performance.

From the point which I call A to the point B is, or ought to be, 5000 yards. At A there is a gap in the wood, and you get a gorgeous view over the valley. The road from La Ferté to the point B runs on high ground, and at B there is a corresponding gap, the road being open completely for roughly 200 yards. A convoy of German lorries was passing with an escort of infantry, and the General thought we might as well have a shot at them. Two 18-pdrs. were man-handled to the side of the hill and opened fire, while six of us with glasses and our lunch sat behind and watched.

It was a dainty sight—the lorries scooting across, while the escort took cover. The guns picked off a few, completely demolishing two lorries, then with a few shells into some cavalry that appeared on the horizon, they ceased fire.

The affair seemed dangerous to the uninitiated despatch rider. Behind the two guns was a brigade of artillery in column of route on an exceedingly steep and narrow road. Guns firing in the open can be seen. If the Germans were to spot us, we shuddered to think what would become of the column behind us on the road.

That afternoon I had nothing more to do, so, returning to the common, I dozed there for a couple of hours, knowing that I should have little sleep that night. At dusk we bivouacked in the garden of the chateau at Méry. We arrived at the chateau before the Staff and picked up some wine.

In the evening I heard that a certain captain in the gunners went reconnoitring and found the battery—it was only one—that had held up our advance. He returned to the General, put up his eyeglass and drawled, "I say, General, I've found that battery. I shall now deal with it." He did. In five minutes it was silenced, and the 14th attacked up the Valley of Death, as the men called it. They were repulsed with very heavy losses; their reinforcements, which had arrived the day before, were practically annihilated.

It was a bad day.

That night it was showery, and I combined vain attempts to get to sleep between the showers with a despatch to 2nd Corps at Saacy and another to the Division Ammunition Column the other side of Charnesseuil.

Towards morning the rain became heavier, so I took up my bed—*i.e.*, my greatcoat and ground-sheet—and, finding four free square feet in the S.O., had an hour's troubled sleep before I was woken up half an hour before dawn to get ready to take an urgent message as soon as it was light.

On September 9th, just before dawn—it was raining and very cold—I was sent with a message to Colonel Cameron at the top of the hill, telling him he might advance. The Germans, it appeared, had retired during the night. Returning to the chateau at Méry, I found the company had gone on, so I followed them along the Valley of Death to Montreuil.

It was the most dismal morning, dark as if the sun would never rise, chequered with little bursts of heavy rain. The road was black with mud. The hedges dripped audibly into watery ditches. There was no grass, only a plentiful coarse vegetation. The valley itself seemed enclosed by unpleasant hills from joy or light. Soldiers lined the road—some were dead, contorted, or just stretched out peacefully; some were wounded, and they moaned as I passed along. There was one officer who slowly moved his head from side to side. That was all he could do. But I could not stop; the ambulances were coming up. So I splashed rapidly through the mud to the cross-roads north of Montreuil.

To the right was a barn in which the Germans had slept. It was littered with their equipment. And in front of it was a derelict motor-car dripping in the rain.

At Montreuil we had a scrap of bully with a bit of biscuit for breakfast, then we ploughed slowly and dangerously alongside the column to Dhuizy, where a house that our artillery had fired was still burning. The chalked billeting marks of the Germans were still on the doors of the cottages. I had a despatch to take back along the column to the Heavies. Grease a couple of inches thick carpeted the road. We all agreed that we should be useless in winter.

At Dhuizy the sun came out.

A couple of miles farther on I had a talk with two German prisoners—R.A.M.C. They were sick of the war. Summed it up thus:

Wir weissen nichts: wir essen nichts: immer laufen, laufen, laufen.

In bright sunshine we pushed on towards Gandeln. On the way we had a bit of lunch, and I left a pipe behind. As there was nothing doing I pushed on past the column, waiting for a moment to watch some infantry draw a large wood, and arrived with the cavalry at Gandeln, a rakish old town at the bottom of an absurdly steep hill. Huggie passed me with a message. Returning he told me that the road ahead was pitiably disgusting.

You must remember that we were hotly pursuing a disorganised foe. In front the cavalry and horse artillery were harassing them for all they were worth, and whenever there was an opening our bigger guns would gallop up for a trifle of blue murder.

From Gandeln the road rises sharply through woods and then runs on high ground without a vestige of cover for two and a half miles into Chézy. On this high, open ground our guns caught a German convoy, and we saw the result.

First there were a few dead and wounded Germans, all muddied. The men would look curiously at each, and sometimes would laugh. Then at the top of the hill we came upon some smashed and abandoned wagons. These were hastily looted. Men piled themselves with helmets, greatcoats, food, saddlery, until we looked a crowd of dishevelled bandits. The German wounded watched—they lay scattered in a cornfield, like poppies. Sometimes Tommy is not a pleasant animal, and I hated him that afternoon. One dead German had his pockets full of chocolate. They scrambled over him, pulling him about, until it was all divided.

Just off the road was a small sandpit. Three or four wagons—the horses, frightened by our shells, had run over the steep place into the sand. Their heads and necks had been forced back into their carcasses, and on top of this mash were the splintered wagons. I sat for a long time by the well in Chézy and watched the troops go by, caparisoned with spoils. I hated war.

Just as the sun was setting we toiled out of Chézy on to an upland of cornfields, speckled with grey patches of dead men and reddish-brown patches of dead horses. One great horse stood out on a little cliff, black against the yellow of the descending sun. It furiously stank. Each time I passed it I held my nose, and I was then pretty well used to smells. The last I saw of it—it lay grotesquely on its back with four stiff legs sticking straight up like the legs of an overturned table—it was being buried by a squad of little black men billeted near. They were cursing richly. The horse's revenge in death, perhaps, for its ill-treatment in life.

It was decided to stay the night at Chézy. The village was crowded, dark, and confusing. Three of us found the signal office, and made ourselves very comfortable for the night with some fresh straw that we piled all over us. The roads were for the first time too greasy for night-riding. The rest slept in a barn near, and did not discover the signal office until dawn.

We awoke, stiff but rested, to a fine warm morning. It was a quiet day. We rode with the column along drying roads until noon through peaceful rolling country—then, as there was nothing doing, Grimers and I rode to the head of the column, and inquiring with care whether our cavalry was comfortably ahead, came to the village of Noroy-sur-Ourcq. We "scrounged" for food and found an inn. At first our host, a fat well-to-do old fellow, said the Germans had taken everything, but, when he saw we really were hungry, he produced sardines, bread, butter, sweets, and good red wine. So we made an excellent meal—and were not allowed to pay a penny.

He told that the Germans, who appeared to be in great distress, had taken everything in the village, though they had not maltreated any one. Their horses were dropping with fatigue—that we knew—and their officers kept telling their men to hurry up and get quickly on the march. At this point they were just nine hours in front of us.

Greatly cheered we picked up the Division again at Chouy, and sat deliciously on a grass bank to wait for the others. Just off the road on the opposite side was a dead German. Quite a number of men broke their ranks to look curiously at him—anything to break the tedious, deadening monotony of marching twenty-five miles day after day: as a major of the Dorsets said to us as we sat there, "It is all right for us, but it's hell for them!"

The Company came up, and we found that in Chouy the Germans had overlooked a telephone—great news for the cable detachment. After a glance at the church, a gorgeous bit of Gothic that we had shelled, we pushed on in the rain to Billy-sur-Ourcq. I was just looking after a convenient loft when I was sent back to Chouy to find the Captain's watch. A storm was raging down the valley. The road at any time was covered with tired foot sloggers. I had to curse them, for they wouldn't get out of the way. Soon I warmed and cursed them crudely and glibly in four languages. On my return I found some looted boiled eggs and captured German Goulasch hot for me. I fed and turned in.

This day my kit was left behind with other unnecessary "tackle," to lighten the horses' load. I wish I had known it.

The remaining eggs for breakfast—delicious.

Huggie and I were sent off just before dawn on a message that took us to St Rémy, a fine church, and Hartennes, where we were given hot tea by that great man, Sergeant Croucher of the Divisional Cyclists. I rode back to Rozet St Albin, a pleasant name, along a road punctuated with dead and very evil-smelling horses. Except for the smell it was a good run of about ten miles. I picked up the Division again on the sandy road above Chacrise.

Sick of column riding I turned off the main road up a steep hill into Ambrief, a desolate black-and-white village totally deserted. It came on to pour, but there was a shrine handy. There I stopped until I was pulled out by an ancient captain of cuirassiers, who had never seen an Englishman before and wanted to hear all about us.

On into Acy, where I decided to head off the Division at Ciry, instead of crossing the Aisne and riding straight to Vailly, our proposed H.Q. for that night. The decision saved my life, or at least my liberty. I rode to Sermoise, a bright little village where the people were actually making bread. At the station there was a solitary cavalry man. In Ciry itself there was no one. Half-way up the Ciry hill, a sort of dry watercourse, I ran into some cavalry and learnt that the Germans were holding the Aisne in unexpected strength. I had all but ridden round and in front of our own cavalry outposts.

Two miles farther back I found Huggie and one of our brigades. We had a bit of bully and biscuit under cover of a haystack, then we borrowed some glasses and watched bodies of Germans on the hills the other side of the Aisne. It was raining very fast. There was no decent cover, so we sat on the leeward side of a mound of sand.

When we awoke the sun was setting gorgeously. Away to the west in the direction of Soissons there was a tremendous cannonade. On the hills opposite little points of flame showed that the Germans were replying. On our right some infantry were slowly advancing in extended order through a dripping turnip-field.

The Battle of the Aisne had begun.

We were wondering what to do when we were commandeered to take a message down that precipitous hill of Ciry to some cavalry. It was now quite dark and still raining. We had no carbide, and my carburettor had jibbed, so we decided to stop at Ciry for the night. At the inn we found many drinks—particularly some wonderful cherry brandy—and a friendly motor-cyclist who told us of a billet that an officer was probably going to leave. We went there. Our host was an old soldier, so, after his wife had hung up what clothes we dared take off to dry by a red-hot stove, he gave us some supper of stewed game and red wine, then made us cunning beds with straw, pillows, and blankets. Too tired to thank him we dropped asleep.

That, though we did not know it then, was the last night of our little Odyssey. We had been advancing or retiring without a break since my tragic farewell to Nadine. We had been riding all day and often all night. But those were heroic days, and now as I write this in our comfortable slack winter quarters, I must confess—I would give anything to have them all over again. Now we motor-cyclists are middle-aged warriors. Adventures are work. Experiences are a routine. Then, let's be sentimental, we were young.

CHAPTER 7

The Battle of the Aisne

I'm going to start by giving you an account of what we thought of the military situation during the great marches and the battle of the Aisne—for my own use. What happened we shall be able to look up afterwards in some lumbersome old history, should we forget, but, unless I get down quickly what we thought, it will disappear in after-knowledge.

You will remember how the night we arrived on the Aisne Huggie and I stretched ourselves on a sand-heap at the side of the road—just above Ciry—and watched dim columns of Germans crawling like grey worms up the slopes the other side of the valley. We were certain that the old Division was still in hot cry on the heels of a rapidly retreating foe. News came—I don't know how: you never do—that our transport and ammunition were being delayed by the fearsome and lamentable state of the roads. But the cavalry was pushing on ahead, and tired infantry were stumbling in extended order through the soaked fields on either side of us. There was hard gunnery well into the red dusk. Right down the valley came the thunder of it, and we began to realise that divisions, perhaps even corps, had come up on either flank.

The ancient captain of cuirassiers, who had hauled me out of my shrine into the rain that afternoon, made me understand there was a great and unknown number of French on our left. From the Order before the Marne I had learnt that a French Army had turned the German right, but the first news I had had of French on our own right was when one staff-officer said in front of me that the French away to the east had been held up. That was at Doué.

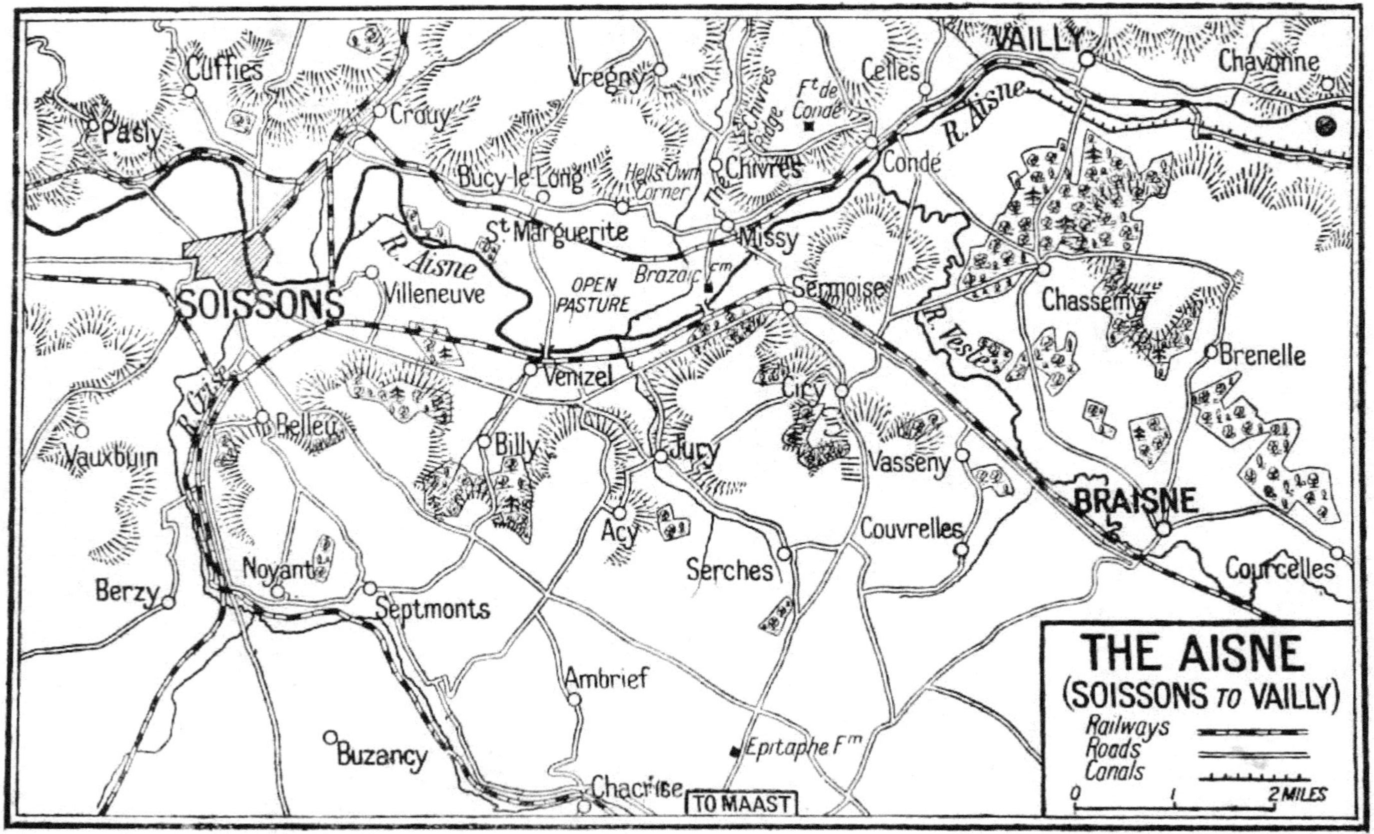
THE AISNE
(SOISSONS TO VAILLY)
Railways
Roads
Canals
0 1 2 MILES
SOISSONS
VAILLY
BRAISNE
R. Aisne
R. Vesle
R. Crise
Cuffies
Pasly
Crouy
Vregny
Bucy-le-Long
Hell's Own Corner
The Chivres Ridge
Chivres
Ft de Condé
Celles
Condé
Chavonne
St. Marguerite
Missy
Brazoic Fm
OPEN PASTURE
Villeneuve
Sermoise
Chassemy
Brenelle
Venizel
Ciry
Belleu
Vauxbuin
Billy
Jury
Vasseny
Acy
Couvrelles
Serches
Courcelles
Noyant
Septmonts
Berzy
Ambrief
Buzancy
Epitaphe Fm
Chacrise
TO MAAST

Our retreat had been solitary. The French, everybody thought, had left us in the lurch at Mons and again at Le Cateau, when the cavalry we knew to be there refused to help us. For all we knew the French Army had been swept off the face of the earth. We were just retiring, and retiring before three or four times our own numbers. We were not even supported by the 1st Corps on our right. It was smashed, and had all it could do to get itself away. We might have been the Ten Thousand.

But the isolation of our desperate retreat dismayed nobody, for we all had an unconquerable belief in the future. There must be some French somewhere, and in spite—as we thought then—of our better judgments, we stuck to the story that was ever being circulated: "We are luring the Germans into a trap." It was impressed upon us, too, by "the Div." that both at Mons and Le Cateau we were strategically victorious. We had given the Germans so hard a knock that they could not pursue us at once; we had covered the retirement of the 1st Corps; we had got away successfully ourselves. We were sullen and tired victors, never defeated. If we retreated, it was for a purpose. If we advanced, the Germans were being crushed.

The Germans thought we were beaten, because they didn't realise we knew we were victorious the whole time.

I do not say that we were always monotonously cheerful. The night after Le Cateau we all thought the game was up—until the morning, when cheerfulness came with the sun. Then we sighed with relief and remembered a little bitterly that we were "luring the Germans on."

Many a time I have come across isolated units in hot corners who did not see a way out. Yet if a battery or a battalion were hard hit, the realisation of local defeat was always accompanied by a fervent faith that "the old Fifth" was doing well. Le Cateau is a victory in the soldier's calendar.

Lè Cateàu and Là Bassèe,
It jolly well serves them right.

We had been ten days or more on the Aisne before we grasped that the force opposite us was not merely a dogged, well-entrenched rearguard, but a section of the German line.

Soon after we arrived a French cavalry officer had ridden into D.H.Q., and after his departure it was freely rumoured that he had ridden right round the German position. News began to trickle in from either flank. Our own attacks ceased, and we took up a defensive position. It was the beginning of trench-warfare, though owing to the nature of the country there were few trenches. Then we heard vaguely that the famous series of enveloping movements had begun, but by this time the Division was tired to death, and the men were craving for a rest.

Strategy in the ranks—it was elementary stuff pieced vaguely together. But perhaps it will interest you at home to know what we thought out here on this great little stage. What we did you have heard. Still, here is the play as we acted in it.

Along the Aisne the line of our Division stretched from Venizel to the bridge of Condé. You must not think of the river as running through a gorge or as meandering along the foot of slopes rising directly from the river bank. On the southern side lie the Heights of Champagne, practically a tableland. From the river this tableland looks like a series of ridges approaching the valley at an angle. Between the foothills and the river runs the Soissons-Rheims road, good *pavé*, and for the most part covered by trees. To the north there is a distance of two miles or so from the river to the hills.

Perhaps I shall make this clearer if I take the three main points about the position.

First. If you are going to put troops on the farther side of the river you must have the means of crossing it, and you must keep those means intact. The bridges running from left to right of our line were at Venizel, Missy, Sermoise, and Condé. The first three were blown up. Venizel bridge was repaired sufficiently to allow of light traffic to cross, and fifty yards farther down a pontoon-bridge was built fit for heavy traffic. Missy was too hot: we managed an occasional ferry. I do not think we ever had a bridge at Sermoise. Once when in search of the C.R.E. I watched a company of the K.O.S.B. being ferried across under heavy rifle fire. The raft was made of ground-sheets stuffed, I think, with straw. Condé bridge the Germans always held, or rather neither of us held it, but the Germans were very close to it and allowed nobody to cross. Just on our side of the bridge was a car containing two dead officers. No one could reach them. There they sat until we left, ghastly sentinels, and for all I know they sit there still.

Now all communication with troops on the north bank of the river had to pass over these bridges, of which Venizel alone was comparatively safe. If ever these bridges should be destroyed, the troops on the north bank would be irrevocably cut off from supplies of every sort and from orders. I often used to wonder what would have happened if the Germans had registered accurately upon the bridges, or if the river had risen and swept the bridges away.

Second. There was an open belt between the river and the villages which we occupied—Bucy-le-Long, St Marguerite, Missy. The road that wound through this belt was without the veriest trace of cover—so much so, that for a considerable time all communication across it was carried on by despatch riders, for a cable could never be laid. So if our across-the-river brigades had ever been forced to retire in daylight they would have been compelled, first to retire two miles over absolutely open country, and then to cross bridges of which the positions were known with tolerable accuracy to the Germans.

Third. On the northern bank four or five spurs came down into the plain, parallel with each other and literally at right angles to the river. The key to these was a spur known as the Chivres hill or plateau. This we found impregnable to the attack of two brigades. It was steep and thickly wooded. Its assailants, too, could be heavily enfiladed from either flank.

Now you have the position roughly. The tactics of our Division were simple. In the early days, when we thought that we had merely a determined rearguard in front of us, we attacked. Bridges—you will remember the tale—were most heroically built. Two brigades (14th and 15th) crossed the river and halted at the very foot of the hills, where they were almost under cover from alien fire. The third brigade was on their right in a position I will describe later.

Well, the two brigades attacked, and attacked with artillery support, but they could not advance. That was the first phase. Then orders came that we were to act on the defensive, and finally of our three brigades, one was on the right, one across the river, and one in a second line of trenches on the southern bank of the river acted as divisional reserve. That for us was the battle of the Aisne. It was hard fighting all through.[13]

Under these conditions there was plentiful work for despatch riders. I am going to try and describe it for you.

When D.H.Q. are stationary, the work of despatch riders is of two kinds. First of all you have to find the positions of the units to which you are sent. Often the Signal Office gives you the most exiguous information. "The 105th Brigade is somewhere near Ciry," or "The Div. Train is at a farm just off the Paris-Bordeaux" road. Starting out with these explicit instructions, it is very necessary to remember that they may be wrong and are probably misleading. That is not the fault of the Signal Office. A Unit changes ground, say from a farm on the road to a farm off the road. These two farms are so near each other that there is no need to inform the Div. just at present of this change of residence. The experienced despatch rider knows that, if he is told the 105th Brigade is at 1904 Farm, the Brigade is probably at 1894 Farm, half a mile away.

Again, a despatch rider is often sent out after a unit has moved and before the message announcing the move has "come through" to the Division.

When the Division is advancing or retiring this exploration-work is the only work. To find a given brigade, take the place at which it was last reported at the Signal Office and assume it was never there. Prefer the information you get from your fellow despatch riders. Then find out the road along which the brigade is said to be moving. If the brigade may be in action, take a road that will bring you to the rear of the brigade. If there are troops in front of the brigade, strike for the head of it. It is always quicker to ride from van to rear of a brigade than from rear to van.

13. I do not pretend for a moment that all these details are meticulously accurate. They are what I knew or thought I knew at the time this was written.

The second kind of work consists in riding along a road already known. A clever despatch rider may reduce this to a fine art. He knows exactly at which corner he is likely to be sniped, and hurries accordingly. He remembers to a yard where the sentries are. If the road is under shell fire, he recalls where the shells usually fall, the interval between the shells and the times of shelling. For there is order in everything, and particularly in German gunnery. Lastly, he does not race along with nose on handle-bar. That is a trick practised only by despatch riders who are rarely under fire, who have come to a strange and alarming country from Corps or Army Headquarters. The experienced motor-cyclist sits up and takes notice the whole time. He is able at the end of his ride to give an account of all that he has seen on the way.

D.H.Q. were at Serches, a wee village in a hollow at the head of a valley. So steeply did the hill rise out of the hollow to the north that the village was certainly in dead ground. A fine road went to the west along the valley for three miles or so to the Soissons-Rheims road. For Venizel you crossed the main road and ran down a little hill through a thick wood, terribly dark of nights, to the village; you crossed the bridge and opened the throttle.

The first time I rode north from Venizel, Moulders was with me. On the left a few hundred yards away an ammunition section that had crossed by the pontoon was at full gallop. I was riding fast—the road was loathsomely open—but not too fast, because it was greasy. A shell pitched a couple of hundred yards off the road, and then others, far enough away to comfort me.

A mile on the road bends sharp left and right over the railway and past a small factory of some sort. The Germans loved this spot, and would pitch shells on it with a lamentable frequency. Soon it became too much of a routine to be effective. On shelling-days three shells would be dropped one after another, an interval of three minutes, and then another three. This we found out and rode accordingly.

A hundred yards past the railway you ride into Bucy-le-Long and safety. The road swings sharp to the right, and there are houses all the way to St Marguerite.

Once I was riding with despatches from D.H.Q. It was a heavy, misty day. As I sprinted across the open I saw shrapnel over St Marguerite, but I could not make out whether it was German shrapnel bursting over the village or our shrapnel bursting over the hills beyond. I slowed down.

Now, as I have told you, on a motor-cycle, if you are going rapidly, you cannot hear bullets or shells coming or even shells bursting unless they are very near. Running slowly on top, with the engine barely turning over, you can hear everything. So I went slow and listened. Through the air came the sharp *woop-wing* of shrapnel bursting towards you, the most devilish sound of all. Some prefer the shriek of shrapnel to the dolorous wail and deep thunderous crash of high explosive. But nothing frightens me so much as the shrapnel-shriek.[14]

Well, as I passed the little red factory I noticed that the shrapnel was bursting right over the village, which meant that as 80 per cent of shrapnel bullets shoot forward the village was comparatively safe. As a matter of fact the street was full of ricocheting trifles.

Transport was drawn up well under cover of the wall and troops were marching in single file as near to the transport as possible. Two horses were being led down the middle of the street. Just before they reached me the nose of one of the horses suddenly was gashed and a stream of blood poured out. Just a ricochet, and it decided me. Despatch riders have to take care of themselves when H.Q. are eight miles away by road and there is no wire. I put my motor-cycle under cover and walked the remaining 200 yards.

Coming back I heard some shouting, a momentary silence, then a flare of the finest blasphemy. I turned the bend to see an officer holding his severed wrist and cursing. He was one of those dashing fellows. He had ridden alongside the transport swearing at the men to get a move on. He had held up his arm to give the signal when a ricochet took his hand off cleanly. His men said not a word—sat with an air of calm disapproval like Flemish oxen.

---

14. Curiously enough, months after this was written the author was wounded by shrapnel.

It was one in the morning and dark on the road when I took my next despatch to St Marguerite. Just out of Bucy I passed Moulders, who shouted, "Ware wire and horses." Since last I had seen it the village had been unmercifully shelled. Where the transport had been drawn up there were shattered wagons. Strewn over the road were dead horses, of all carcasses the most ludicrously pitiful, and wound in and out of them, a witches' web, crawled the wire from the splintered telegraph posts. There was not a sound in the village except the gentle thump of my engine. I was forced to pull up, that I might more clearly see my way between two horses. My engine silent, I could only hear a little whisper from the house opposite and a dripping that I did not care to understand. Farther on a house had fallen half across the road. I scarcely dared to start my engine again in the silence of this desolate destruction. Then I could not, because the dripping was my petrol and not the gore of some slaughtered animal. A flooded carburettor is a nuisance in an unsavoury village.

At the eastern end of St Marguerite the road turns sharply south. This is "Hell's Own Corner." From it there is a full and open view of the Chivres valley, and conversely those in the Chivres valley can see the corner very clearly. When we were acting on the offensive, a section of 4.5 in. howitzers were put into position just at the side of the road by the corner. This the Germans may have discovered, or perhaps it was only that the corner presented a tempting target, for they shelled to destruction everything within a hundred yards. The howitzers were rapidly put out of action though not destroyed, and a small orchard just behind them was ploughed, riven, and scarred with high explosive and shrapnel.

The day St Marguerite was shelled one of the two brigadiers determined to shift his headquarters to a certain farm. N'Soon and Grimers were attached to the brigade at the time. "Headquarters" came to the corner. N'Soon and Grimers were riding slowly in front. They heard a shell coming. Grimers flung himself off his bicycle and dropped like a stone. N'Soon opened his throttle and darted forward, foolishly. The shell exploded. Grimers' bicycle was covered with branches and he with earth and dust. N'Soon for some reason was not touched.

The General and his staff were shelled nearly the whole way to the farm, but nobody was hit. The brigade veterinary officer had a theory that the safest place was next the General, because generals were rarely hit, but that day his faith was shaken, and the next day—I will tell you the story—it tottered to destruction.

I had come through St Marguerite the night after the brigade had moved. Of course I was riding without a light. I rounded Hell's Own Corner carefully, very frightened of the noise my engine was making. A little farther on I dismounted and stumbled to the postern-gate of a farm. I opened it and went in. A sentry challenged me in a whisper and handed me over to an orderly, who led me over the black bodies of men sleeping to a lean-to where the General sat with a sheltered light, talking to his staff. He was tired and anxious. I delivered my despatch, took the receipted envelope and stumbled back to the postern-gate. Silently I hauled my motor-cycle inside, then started on my tramp to the General who had moved.

After Hell's Own Corner the road swings round again to the east, and runs along the foot of the Chivres hill to Missy. A field or so away to the left is a thick wood inhabited for the most part by German snipers. In the preceding days N'Soon and Sadders had done fine work along this road in broad daylight, carrying despatches to Missy.

I was walking, because no motor-cyclist goes by night to a battalion, and the noise of a motor-cycle would have advertised the presence of brigade headquarters somewhere on the road. It was a joyous tramp of two miles into the village of dark, ominous houses. I found a weary subaltern who put me on my way, a pitch-black lane between high walls. At the bottom of it I stepped upon an officer, who lay across the path asleep with his men. So tired was he that he did not wake. On over a field to the farm. I delivered my despatch to the Brigade-Major, whose eyes were glazed with want of sleep. He spoke to me in the pitiful monotone of the unutterably weary. I fed off bully, hot potatoes, bread and honey, then turned in.

In the morning I had just finished my breakfast when a shell exploded fifty yards behind the farm, and others followed. "Headquarters" turned out, and we crawled along a shallow ditch at the side of a rough country road until we were two hundred yards from the farm. We endeavoured to get into communication with the other brigade by flag, but after the first message a shell dropped among the farther signallers and we saw no more of them.

Shells began to drop near us. One fellow came uncomfortably close. It covered us with dirt as we "froze" to the bottom of the ditch. A little scrap of red-hot metal flew into the ground between me and the signal sergeant in front of me. I grabbed it, but dropped it because it was so hot; it was sent to the signal sergeant's wife and not to you.

We crawled a hundred yards farther along to a place where the ditch was a little deeper, and we were screened by some bushes, but I think the General's red hat must have been marked down, because for the next hour we lay flat listening to the zip-zip of bullets that passed barely overhead.

Just before we moved the Germans started to shell Missy with heavy howitzers. Risking the bullets, we saw the village crowned with great lumps of smoke. Our men poured out of it in more or less extended order across the fields. I saw them running, poor little khaki figures, and dropping like rabbits to the rifles of the snipers in the wood.

Two hundred yards south of the St Marguerite-Missy road—that is, between the road and the ditch in which we were lying—there is a single line of railway on a slight embankment. Ten men in a bunch made for the cover it afforded. One little man with an enormous pack ran a few yards in front. Seven reached the top of the embankment, then three almost simultaneously put their hands before their eyes and dropped across the rails. The little man ran on until he reached us, wide-eyed, sweaty, and breathing in short gasps. The Brigade-Major shouted to him not to come along the road but to make across the field. Immediately the little man heard the voice of command he halted, stood almost to attention, and choked out, "But they're shelling us"—then, without another word he turned off across the fields and safely reached cover.

In the ditch we were comfortable if confined, and I was frightened when the order came down, "Pass the word for the motor-cyclist." I crawled up to the General, received my despatch, and started walking across the field. Then I discovered there is a great difference between motor-cycling under rifle fire, when you can hear only the very close ones, and walking across a heavy turnip-field when you can hear all. Two-thirds of the way a sharp zip at the back of my neck and a remembrance of the three men stretched across the rails decided me. I ran.

At the farm where the other brigade headquarters were stationed I met Sadders with a despatch for the general I had just left. When I explained to him where and how to go he blenched a little, and the bursting of a shell a hundred yards or so away made him jump, but he started off at a good round pace. You must remember we were not used to carrying despatches on foot.

I rode lazily through St Marguerite and Bucy-le-Long, and turned the corner on to the open stretch. There I waited to allow a battery that was making the passage to attract as many shells as it liked. The battery reached Venizel with the loss of two horses. Then, just as I was starting off, a shell plunged into the ground by the little red factory. As I knew it to be the first of three I waited again.

At that moment Colonel Seely's car came up, and Colonel Seely himself got out and went forward with me to see if the road had been damaged. For three minutes the road should have been safe, but the German machine became human, and in a couple of minutes Colonel Seely and I returned covered with rich red plough and with a singing in our ears. I gave the Colonel a couple of hundred yards start, and we sprinted across into the safe hands of Venizel.

Beyond Missy, which we intermittently occupied, our line extended along the foot of the hills and crossed the Aisne about three-quarters of a mile short of Condé bridge—and that brings me to a tale.

One night we were healthily asleep after a full day. I had been "next for duty" since ten o'clock, but at two I began to doze, because between two and five there is not often work for the despatch rider. At three I awoke to much shouting and anxious hullabaloo. The intelligence officer was rousing us hurriedly—"All motor-cyclists turn out. Pack up kit. Seven wanted at once in the Signal Office."

This meant, firstly, that Divisional Headquarters were to move at once, in a hurry, and by night; secondly, that the same despatch was to be sent simultaneously to every unit in the Division. I asked somebody to get my kit together, and rushed upstairs to the Signal Office. There on the table I saw the fateful wire.

"Germans entrenched south side of Condé bridge and are believed to be crossing in large numbers." I was given a copy of this message to take to the 15th Brigade, then at St Marguerite. Away on the road at full speed I thought out what this meant. The enemy had broken through our line—opposite Condé there were no reserves—advance parties of the Germans might even now be approaching headquarters—large numbers would cut us off from the Division on our right and would isolate the brigade to which I was going; it would mean another Le Cateau.

I tore along to Venizel, and slowing down at the bridge shouted the news to the officer in charge—full speed across the plain to Bucy, and caring nothing for the sentries' shouts, on to St Marguerite. I dashed into the general's bedroom and aroused him. Almost before I had arrived the general and his brigade-major—both in pyjamas—were issuing commands and writing messages. Sleepy and amazed orderlies were sent out at the double. Battalion commanders and the C.R.E. were summoned.

I started back for D.H.Q. with an acknowledgment, and rattling through the village came out upon the plain.

Over Condé bridge an ochreous, heavy dawn broke sullenly. There was no noise of firing to tell me that the men of our right brigade were making a desperate resistance to a fierce advance. A mile from Serches I passed a field-ambulance loaded up for instant flight; the men were standing about in little groups talking together, as if without orders. At Headquarters I found that a despatch rider had been sent hot-foot to summon two despatch riders, who that night were with the corps, and others to every unit. Everybody carried the same command—load up and be ready to move at a moment's notice.

Orders to move were never sent. Our two ghastly sentinels still held the bridge. It was a scare.

The tale that we heard at the time was the tale of a little German firing—a lost patrol of ours, returning by an unauthorised road, mistaken in the mist for Germans—a verbal message that had gone wrong. As for the lieutenant who—it was said—first started the hare, his name was burnt with blasphemy for days and days. The only men who came out of it well were some of our cyclists, who, having made their nightly patrol up to the bridge, returned just before dawn to D.H.Q. and found the Division trying to make out that it had not been badly frightened.

I did not hear what really happened at the bridge that night until I published my paper, "The Battle of the Aisne," in the May 'Blackwood.' Here is the story as I had it from the officer principally concerned—

Condé bridge was under our control by shell-fire alone, so that we were obliged to patrol its unpleasant neighbourhood by night. For this purpose an "officer's patrol" was organised (in addition to the "standing patrol" provided by the Cyclists) and supplied every night by different battalions. So many conflicting reports were received nightly about the bridge that the officer who told me the story was appointed Brigade Patrolling Officer.

He established himself in a certain wood, and on the night in question worked right up beyond Condé bridge—until he found a burning house about 200 yards beyond the bridge on the south side of it. In the flare of the house he was surprised to discover Germans entrenched in an old drain on the British side of the river. He had unknowingly passed this body of the enemy.

He heard, too, a continuous stream of Germans in the transport marching through the woods towards the bridge. Working his way back, he reported the matter personally to the Brigadier of the 13th, who sent the famous message to the Division.

It appears that the Germans had come down to fill their water-carts that night, and to guard against a surprise attack had pushed forward two platoons across the bridge into the drain. Unfortunately one of our patrols disobeyed its orders that night and patrolled a forbidden stretch of road. The officer shot two of these men in the dark.

Three days later the outpost company on Vesle bridge of the Aisne was surrounded, and, later still, Condé bridge passed out of our artillery control, and was finally crossed by the Germans.

I have written of this famous scare of Condé bridge in detail, not because it was characteristic, but because it was exceptional. It is the only scare we ever had in our Division, and amongst those who were on the Aisne, and are still with the Division, it has become a phrase for encouragement—"Only another Condé."

During the first days on this monotonous river, the days when we attacked, the staff of our right brigade advanced for a time into open country and took cover behind the right haystack of three. To this brigade Huggie took a message early one morning, and continued to take messages throughout the day because—this was his excuse—he knew the road. It was not until several months later that I gathered by chance what had happened on that day, for Huggie, quite the best despatch rider in our Division, would always thwart my journalistic curiosity by refusing resolutely to talk about himself. The rest of us swopped yarns of an evening.

These haystacks were unhealthy: so was the approach to them. First one haystack was destroyed. The brigade went to the next. This second was blown to bits. The staff took refuge behind the third. In my letters I have told you of the good things the other despatch riders in our Division have done, but to keep up continuous communication all day with this be-shelled and refugee brigade was as fine a piece of despatch riding as any. It received its proper reward, as you know.

Afterwards the brigade emigrated to a hillside above Ciry, and remained there. Now the German gunner in whose sector Ciry was included should not be dismissed with a word. He was a man of uncertain temper and accurate shooting, for in the first place he would shell Ciry for a few minutes at any odd time, and in the second he knocked a gun out in three shells and registered accurately, when he pleased, upon the road that led up a precipitous hill to the edge of the Serches hollow. On this hill he smashed some regimental transport to firewood and killed a dozen horses, and during one of his sudden shellings of the village blew a house to pieces just as a despatch rider, who had been told the village that morning was healthy, rode by.

You must not think that we were for ever scudding along, like the typical "motor-cyclist scout" in the advertisements, surrounded with shells. There was many a dull ride even to Bucy-le-Long. An expedition to the Div. Train (no longer an errant and untraceable vagabond) was safe and produced jam. A ride to Corps Headquarters was only dangerous because of the innumerable and bloodthirsty sentries surrounding that stronghold.

One afternoon a report came through to the Division that a motor-car lay derelict at Missy. So "the skipper" called for two volunteers who should be expert mechanics. Divisional Signal companies were not then provided with cars, and if the C.O. wished to go out to a brigade, which might be up to or over eight miles away, he was compelled to ride a horse, experiment with a motor-cycle that was probably badly missed by the despatch riders, or borrow one of the staff cars. Huggie and the elder Cecil volunteered.

As soon as it was dusk they rode down to Sermoise, and crossing by the ferry—it was perilous in the dark—made their way with difficulty across country to Missy, which was then almost in front of our lines. They found the car, and examining it discovered that to outward appearance it was sound—a great moment when after a turn or two of the handle the engine roared into the darkness, but the noise was alarming enough because the Germans were none too far away.

They started on their journey home—by St Marguerite and Venizel. Just after they had left the village the beam of an alien searchlight came sweeping along the road. Before the glare had discovered their nakedness they had pulled the car to the side of the road under the shelter of the hedge nearest the Germans, and jumping down had taken cover. By all the rules of the game it was impossible to drive a car that was not exactly silent along the road from Missy to Hell's Own Corner. The searchlight should have found them, and the fire of the German snipers should have done the rest. But their luck was in, and they made no mistakes. Immediately the beam had passed they leaped on to the car and tore scathless into St Marguerite and so back to the Division.

After its capture the car was exhibited with enormous pride to all that passed by. We should not have been better pleased if we had captured the whole Prussian Guard. For prisoners disappear and cannot always be shown to prove the tale.

In the morning we rode down into Sermoise for the motor-cycles. Sermoise had been shelled to pieces, but I shall never forget a brave and obstinate inhabitant who, when a shell had gone through his roof and demolished the interior of his house, began to patch his roof with bully-tins and biscuit-tins that he might at least have shelter from the rain.

Elated with our capture of the car we scented greater victories. We heard of a motor-boat on the river near Missy, and were filled with visions of an armoured motor-boat, stuffed with machine-guns, plying up and down the Aisne. Huggie and another made the excursion. The boat was in an exposed and altogether unhealthy position, but they examined it, and found that there was no starting-handle. In the village forge, which was very completely fitted up, they made one that did not fit, and then another, but however much they coaxed, the engine would not start. So regretfully they left it.

To these adventures there was a quiet background of uncomfortable but pleasant existence. Life on the Aisne was like a "reading party"—only instead of working at our books we worked at soldiering.

The night that Huggie and I slept down at Ciry, the rest of the despatch riders, certain that we were taken, encamped at Ferme d'Epitaphe, for the flooded roads were impassable. There we found them in the morning, and discovered they had prepared the most gorgeous stew of all my recollection.

Now, to make a good stew is a fine art, for a stew is not merely a conglomeration of bully and vegetables and water boiled together until it looks nice. First the potatoes must be cut out to a proper size and put in; of potatoes there cannot be too many. As for the vegetables, a superfluity of carrots is a burden, and turnips should be used with a sparing hand. A full flavour of leek is a great joy. When the vegetables are nearly boiled, the dixie should be carefully examined by all to see if it is necessary to add water. If in doubt spare the water, for a rich thick gravy is much to be desired. Add bully, and get your canteens ready.

This particular stew made by Orr was epic. At all other good stews it was recalled and discussed, but never did a stew come up to the stew that we so scrupulously divided among us on the bright morning of Sept. 12, 1914, at Ferme d'Epitaphe, above Serches.

Later in the day we took over our billet, a large bicycle shed behind the school in which D.H.Q. were installed. The front of it was open, the floor was asphalt, the roof dripped, and we shared it with the Divisional Cyclists. So close were we packed that you could not turn in your sleep without raising a storm of curses, and if you were called out of nights you were compelled to walk boldly over prostrate bodies, trusting to luck that you did not step on the face of a man who woke suddenly and was bigger than yourself.

On the right of our dwelling was a little shed that was once used as a guard-room. A man and woman were brought in under suspicion of espionage. The woman was put in the shed. There she shrieked the night through, shouted for her husband (he had an ugly-sounding name that we could not understand), and literally tore her hair. The language of the Cyclists was an education even to the despatch riders, who once had been told by their Quartermaster-Sergeant that they left the cavalry standing. Finally, we petitioned for her removal, and once again slept peacefully. The Court of Inquiry found the couple were not spies, but unmarried. So it married them and let them go.

The Cyclists were marvellous and indefatigable makers of tea. At any unearthly hour you might be gently shaken by the shoulder and a voice would whisper—

"'Ave a drop o' tea—real 'ot and plenty o' sugar."

Never have I come back from a night ride without finding

a couple of cyclists squatting out in the gloom round a little bright fire of their own making, with some fine hot tea. Wherever they go may they never want a drink!

And never shall I forget that fine bit of roast pork my friend Sergeant Croucher insisted on sharing with me one evening! I had not tasted fresh meat for weeks.

George was our unofficial Quartermaster. He was and is a great man, always cheerful, able to coax bread, vegetables, wine, and other luxuries out of the most hardened old Frenchwoman; and the French, though ever pathetically eager to do anything for us, always charged a good round price. Candles were a great necessity, and could not be bought, but George always had candles for us. I forget at the moment whether they were for *"Le General French, qui arrive,"* or *"Les pauvres, pauvres, blessés."* On two occasions George's genius brought him into trouble, for military law consists mainly of the commandment—*Thou shalt not allow thyself to be found out.*

We were short of firewood. So George discovered that his engine wanted a little tuning, and started out on a voyage of discovery. Soon he came upon a heap of neatly cut, neatly piled wood. He loaded up until he heard shouts, then fled. That night we had a great fire, but in the morning came tribulation. The shouts were the shouts of the C.R.E. and the wood was an embryonic bridge. Severely reprimanded.

Then there was the Honey Question. There were bees in the village and we had no honey. The reputation of George was at stake. So one night we warily and silently approached some hives with candles; unfortunately we were interfered with by the military police. Still an expedition into the hedgerows and woods always had an excuse in time of war, and we made it.

The village of Acy, high on the hill above the road to Venizel, was the richest hunting-ground. First, there was a bread-shop open at certain hours. George was often late, and, disdaining to take his place in the long line of those who were not despatch riders, would march straight in and demand bread for one of his two worthy charities. When these were looked upon with suspicion he engineered a very friendly understanding with the baker's wife.

Then there was a dark little shop where you could buy good red wine, and beyond it a farmer with vegetables to sell. But his greatest find was the chateau, which clung to the edge of the hill and overlooked the valley of the Aisne to Condé Fort and the Hill of Chivres.

Searching one morning amongst a pile of captured and derelict stuff we discovered a canvas bath. Now, not one of us had had a bath since Havre, so we made arrangements. Three of us took the bath up to the chateau, then inhabited by a caretaker and his wife. They brought us great pails of hot water, and for the first time in a month we were clean. Then we had tea and talked about the Germans who had passed through. The German officer, the old woman told us, had done them no harm, though he had seized everything without paying a *sou*. Just before he left bad news was brought to him. He grew very angry, and shouted to her as he rode off—

"You shall suffer for this when we return;" but she laughed and shouted back at him, mocking—

"When you return!"

And then the English came.

After tea we smoked our pipes in the terraced garden, watched the Germans shelling one of our aeroplanes, examined the German lines, and meditated in safety on the war just like newspaper correspondents.

It was in Serches itself that George received the surprise of his life. He was after potatoes, and seeing a likely-looking old man pass, D.H.Q. ran after him. In his best French—"*Avez-vous pommes-de-terre à vendre?»*

The old man turned round, smiled, and replied in broadest Yorkshire, "Wanting any 'taters?"

George collapsed.

It seems that the old fellow had settled in Serches years and years before. He had a very pretty daughter, who spoke a delectable mixture of Yorkshire and the local dialect. Of course she was suspected of being a spy—in fact, probably was—so the military police were set to watch her—a job, I gathered later from one of them, much to their liking.

Our life on the Aisne, except for little exciting episodes, was restful enough. We averaged, I should think, a couple of day messages and one each night, though there were intermittent periods of high pressure. We began to long for the strenuous first days, and the Skipper, finding that we were becoming unsettled, put us to drill in our spare time and gave some of us riding lessons. Then came rumours of a move to a rest-camp, probably back at Compiègne. The 6th Division arrived to take over from us, or so we were told, and Rich and Cuffe came over with despatches. We had not seen them since Chatham. They regarded us as veterans, and we told them the tale.

One afternoon some artillery of this division came through the valley. They were fine and fresh, but not a single one of us believed they equalled ours. There was a line of men to watch them pass, and everybody discovered a friend until practically at every stirrup there was a man inquiring after a pal, answering questions, and asking what they thought in England, and how recruiting was going. The air rang with crude, great-hearted jokes. We motor-cyclists stood aside just criticising the guns and men and horses. We felt again that shyness we had felt at Chatham in front of the professional soldier. Then we remembered that we had been through the Retreat and the Advance, and went back to tea content.

CHAPTER 8

The Move to the North

We left Serches at dusk with little regret and pushed on over the hill past Ferme d'Epitaphe of gluttonous memory, past the Headquarter clerks, who were jogging peacefully along on bicycles, down the other side of the hill, and on to the village of Maast.

Headquarters were in a curious farm. One side of its court was formed by a hill in which there were caves—good shelter for the men. There was just one run that night to Corps H.Q. in a chateau three miles farther on.

The morning was clear and sunny. A good, lazy breakfast preluded a great wash. Then we chatted discreetly with a Paris *midinette* at the gate of the farm. Though not in Flanders, she was of the Flemish type—bright colouring, high cheek-bones, dark eyes. On these little social occasions—they came all too rarely; that is why I always mention them—there was much advantage in being only a corporal. Officers, even Staff Officers, as they passed threw at us a look of admiration and envy. A salute was cheap at the price.

In the afternoon there was a run, and when I returned I found that the rest-camp rumour had been replaced by two others—either we were going into action immediately a little farther along the line beyond Soissons, or we were about to make a dash to Ostend for the purpose of outflanking the Germans.

We moved again at dusk, and getting clear of the two brigades with H.Q. rode rapidly twenty miles across country, passing over the road by which we had advanced, to Longpont, a big dark chateau set in a wood and with a French sentry at the gate. Our third brigade was trekking away into the darkness as we came in. We slept in a large room on straw mattresses—very comforting to the bones.

The morning was again gorgeous, and again we breakfasted late and well. The *chateau* we discovered to be monumental, and beside it, set in a beautiful garden, was a ruined chapel, where a service was held—the first we had been able to attend since the beginning of the war.

Our host, an old man, thin and lithe, and dressed in shiny black, came round during the day to see that we had all we needed. We heard a tale—I do not know how true it was—that the Crown Prince had stayed at the chateau. He had drunk much ancient and good wine, and what he had not drunk he had taken away with him, together with some objects of art. The chateau was full of good things.

During the day I had a magnificent run of forty miles over straight dry roads to Hartennes, where, if you will remember, that great man, Sergeant Croucher of the cyclists, had given us tea, and on to Chacrise and Maast. It was the first long and open run I had had since the days of the retreat, when starting from La Pommeraye I had ridden through the forest to Compiègne in search of the Divisional Train.

Just after I had returned we started off again—at dusk. I was sent round to a place, the name of which I cannot remember, to a certain division; then I struck north along a straight road through the forest to Villers-Cotterets. The town was crammed with French motor-lorries and crowded with French troops, who greeted me hilariously as I rode through to Véze.

There we slept comfortably in the lodge of the chateau, all, that is, except Grimers, who had been seized with a puncture just outside the main hotel in Villers-Cotterets.

In the morning I had a fine run to a brigade at Béthancourt, the little village, you will remember, where we lunched off an excellent omelette, and convinced the populace, with the help of our host, that the Germans would come no farther.

While I was away the rest discovered some excellent white wine in the cellar of the lodge, and before starting again at dusk we made a fine meal. Cecil and I remained after the others had gone, and when the wife of the lodge-keeper came in and expressed her utter detestation of all troops, we told her that we were shedding our blood for France, and offered her forgetfully a glass of her own good wine.

That night we slept at Béthisy St Martin. On the retreat, you will remember, the lord of the chateau had given some of the despatch riders dinner, before they learnt that D.H.Q. had been diverted to Crécy-en-Valois. He recognised us with joy, allowed us to take things from the kitchen, and in the morning hunted out for us a tennis set. Four of us who were not on duty played a great game on a very passable gravel court.

We now heard that "the Division" was convinced that we were going to make a dash for Ostend, and rumour seemed to crystallise into truth when orders came that we were to entrain that night at Pont St Maxence.

The despatch riders rode ahead of the column, and received a joyous welcome in the town. We stalked bravely into a café, and drank loud and hearty toasts with some friendly but rather drunk French soldiers. Gascons they were, and d'Artagnans all, from their proper boasting—the heart of a lion and the cunning of a fox, they said. One of us was called into a more sober chamber to drink ceremonious toasts in champagne with their officers. In the street another of us—I would not give even his initial—selecting the leading representative of young, demure, and ornamental maidenhood, embraced her in the middle of the most admiring crowd I have ever seen, while the rest of us explained to a half-angry mother that her daughter should be proud and happy—as indeed she was—to represent the respectable and historic town of Pont St Maxence.

Then, amidst shrieks and cheers and cries of "Brave Tommy" and "We love you," the despatch riders of the finest and most famous of all Divisions rode singing to the station, where we slept peacefully on straw beside a large fire until the train came in and the Signal Company arrived.

Our entraining at Pont St Maxence began with a carouse and ended with a cumulative disappointment. In the middle was the usual wait, a tiresome but necessary part of all military evolutions. To entrain a Signal Company sounds so simple. Here is the company—there is the train. But first comes the man-handling of cable-carts on to trucks that were built for the languid conveyance of perambulators. Then follows a little horseplay, and only those who, like myself, regard horses as unmechanical and self-willed instruments of war, know how terrifying a sight and how difficult a task the emboxing of a company's horses can be. Motor-cycles are heavy and have to be lifted, but they do not make noises and jib and rear, and look every moment as if they were going to fall backward on to the interested spectator.

We despatch riders fetched a great deal of straw and made ourselves comfortable in one of those wagons that are marked outside, with such splendid optimism—

Chevaux 8
Hommes 40-5

With our friend the Post-Sergeant and his underling there were roughly a dozen of us and no superfluity of space, but, seeing men wandering fiercely up and down the train under the command of our Sergeant-Major, we took in a H.Q. clerk. This ruffled us, but it had to be done. The Sergeant-Major came to our wagon. We stood at the door and pointed out to him that we had in our wagon not only all the despatch riders, but also the whole of the Postal and Headquarters Staffs. He said nothing to us—only told ten more men to get in. Finally we were twenty-five in all, with full equipment. Thinking of the 40-5 we settled down and managed to effect a compromise of room which, to our amazement, left us infinitely more comfortable than we had been in the train coming up from Havre to Landrecies.

The train shuffled out of the station just before dawn. We slept a bit, and then, just as it was getting light, started our pipes and began to talk of the future.

The general opinion favoured Ostend, though a sergeant hazarded that we were going to be shipped swiftly across to England to defend the East Coast. This suggestion was voted impossible and tactless—at least, we didn't put it quite like that.

Ostend it was going to be—train to Abbéville, and then boat to Ostend, and a rapid march against the German flank.

The discussion was interrupted by somebody saying he had heard from somebody who had been told by his Major, that 60,000 Germans had been killed in the last two days, Von Kluck had been killed by a lucky shell, and the Crown Prince had committed suicide. We were bringing the cynicism of youth to bear on the trustfulness of a mature mercenary when the train arrived at Amiens.

Some washed. Some meditated on a train of French wounded and another train of Belgian refugees, humble and pitiful objects, very smelly. Two, not waiting for orders, rushed to the buffet and bought beer and sardines and chocolate and bread. One of these was cut off from his wagon by a long goods train that passed through, but he knew the ways of military trains, waited till the goods had passed, then ran after us and caught us up after a mile's jog-trot. The good people of Amiens, who had not so very long before been delivered from the Germans, were exceedingly affectionate, and threw us fruit, flowers, and kisses. Those under military age shrieked at the top of their shrill little trebles—*Engleesh—Tipperary—Biskeet—Biskeet—Souvenir.*

We have never understood the cry of *"Biskeet."* The fat little fellows were obviously well nourished. Perhaps, dog-like, they buried their biscuits with a thought for the time when the English should be forgotten and hunger should take their place as something very present.

So joyously we were rushed north at about five miles an hour, or eight kilometres per hour, which sounds better. Early in the afternoon we came to Abbéville, a hot and quiet station, and, with the aid of some London Scottish, disembarked. From these Scots we learnt that the French were having a rough time just north of Arras, that train-load upon train-load of wounded had come through, that our Corps (the 2nd) was going up to help.

So even now we do not know whether we really were going to Ostend and were diverted to the La Bassée district to help the French who had got themselves into a hole, or whether Ostend was somebody's little tale.

We rode through the town to the Great Barracks, where we were given a large and clean ward. The washing arrangements were sumptuous and we had truckle-beds to sleep upon, but the sanitation, as everywhere in France, was vile. We kicked a football about on the drill-ground. Then some of us went down into the town, while the rest of us waited impatiently for them to come back, taking a despatch or two in the meanwhile.

From the despatch rider's point of view Abbéville is a large and admiring town, with good restaurants and better baths. These baths were finer than the baths of Havre—full of sweet-scented odours and the deliciously intoxicating fumes of good soap and plenteous boiling-water.

In a little restaurant we met some friends of the 3rd Division and a couple of London Scots, who were getting heartily sick of the L. of C., though taking prisoners round the outskirts of Paris had, I gather, its charm even for the most ardent warriors.

In the morning there was parade, a little football, and then a stroll into the town. I had just finished showing an Intelligence Officer how to get a belt back on to the pulley of his motor-cycle when Cecil met me and told me we were to move north that evening.

We had a delectable little tea, bought a map or two, and then strolled back to the barracks. In half an hour we were ready to move off, kit piled high upon our carriers, looking for all the world (said our C.O.) like those funny little animals that carry their houses upon their backs and live at the bottom of ponds. Indeed it was our boast that—such was our ingenuity—we were able to carry more kit than any regimental officer.

It was dusk when N'Soon and I pushed off—we had remained behind to deal with messages that might come in foolishly after the Division had left. We took the great highroad to Calais, and, carefully passing the General, who was clattering along with his staff and an escort of Hussars, we pulled up to light our lamps at a little estaminet with glowing red blinds just like the blinds of certain hospitable taverns in the city of Oxford. The coincidence was so remarkable that we were compelled to enter.

We found a roaring, leaping log-fire, a courteous old Frenchman who drank our health, an immense omelette, some particularly good coffee, and the other despatch riders.

That night it was freezing hard. With our chairs drawn in close to the fire, a glass of something to keep the cold out ready to hand, and pipes going strong, we felt sorry for the general and his escort who, probably with chilled lips and numbed fingers, jogged resoundingly through the village street.

Twenty minutes later we took the road, and soon, pretending that we had lost our way, again passed the general—and lost our way, or at least rode well past our turning. Finally, colder than we had ever been before, we reached the Chateau at Gueschart. There we found a charming and hospitable son of the house and a pleasantly adoring lad. With their aid we piled the floor of the harness-room with straw, and those of us who were not on duty slept finely.

From the dawn of the next morning we were working at top pressure right through the day, keeping in touch with the brigades which were billeted in villages several miles distant.

Late in the afternoon we discovered we were very short of petrol, so I was sent off to Crécy in our famous captured car, with a requisition. We arrived amidst cheers. I strode into the nearest garage and demanded 100 litres of petrol. It was humbly brought and placed in the car: then I sent boys flying round the town for jam and bread and butter, and in the meantime we entertained the crowd by showing them a German helmet. I explained volubly that my bandaged fingers—there was an affair of outposts with an ambulance near Serches—were the work of shrapnel, and they nearly embraced me. A boy came back and said there was no jam, so the daughter of the house went to her private cupboard and brought me out two jars of jam she had made herself, and an enormous glass of wine. We drove off amidst more cheers, to take the wrong road out of the town in our great excitement.

The brigades moved that night; headquarters remained at Gueschart until dawn, when the general started off in his car with two of us attendant.

Now before the war a motor-cyclist would consider himself ill-used if he were forced to take a car's dust for a mile or so. Your despatch rider was compelled to follow in the wake of a large and fast Daimler for twenty-five miles, and at the end of it he did not know which was him and which dust.

We came upon the 15th, shivering in the morning cold, and waiting for some French motor-buses. Then we rushed on to St Pol, which was crammed full of French transport, and on to Chateau Bryas. Until the other despatch riders came up there was no rest for the two of us that had accompanied the car. The roads, too, were blocked with refugees flying south from Lille and men of military age who had been called up. Once again we heard the distant sound of guns—for the first time since we had been at the Chateau of Longpont.

At last we were relieved for an hour, and taking possession of a kitchen we fried some pork-chops with onions and potatoes. It was grand. We washed them down with coffee, and went back to duty. For the remainder of that day and for the whole of the night there was no rest for us.

At dawn the Division marched in column of route north-east towards the sound of the guns.

Half of us at a time slipped away and fed in stinking taverns—but the food was good.

I cannot remember a hotter day, and we were marching through a thickly-populated mining district—the villages were uncomfortably like those round Dour. The people were enthusiastic and generous with their fruit and with their chocolate. It was very tiring work, because we were compelled to ride with the Staff, for first one of us was needed and then another to take messages up and down the column or across country to brigades and divisions that were advancing along roads parallel to ours. The old Division was making barely one mile an hour. The road was blocked by French transport coming in the opposite direction, by buses drawn up at the side of the road, and by cavalry that, trekking from the Aisne, crossed our front continuously to take up their position away on the left.

At last, about three o'clock in the afternoon, we reached the outskirts of Béthune. The sound of the guns was very near, and to the east of the town we could see an aeroplane haloed in bursting shrapnel.

The Staff took refuge first in an unsavoury field and afterwards in a little house. Despatch after despatch until evening—and then, ordered to remain behind to direct others, and cheered by the sight of our most revered and most short-sighted staff-officer walking straight over a little bridge into a deep, muddy, and stinking ditch, I took refuge in the kitchen and experienced the discreeter pleasures of "the Force." The handmaidens brought coffee, and brushed me and washed me and talked to me. I was sorry when the time came for me to resume my beat, or rather to ride with Cecil after the Division.

We passed some Turcos, happy-looking children but ill companions in a hostile country, and some Spahis with flowing *burnous*, who looked ridiculously out of place, and then, after a long search—it was dark on the road and very cold—we found the Division.

I dined off a *maconochie*, and was wondering whether I dare lie down to sleep, when I was called out to take a message to and remain at the 13th Brigade. It was a bad night. Never was a man so cold in his life, and the brigade had taken up its quarters in a farm situated in the centre of a very labyrinth of country roads. But I had four hours' sleep when I got there, while the others were up all the night.

There was no hurry in the morning. The orders were to join the Division at a bridge just outside Béthune, a point which they could not possibly reach before ten. So I got up late and had a glorious meal of soup, omelette, and fruit in the town, waited on by a most excellent flapper who wanted to know everything about everything. I reported at the Signal Office, then occupying the lodge of the town cemetery, and was sent off to catch the Devons. At the village where I waited for them I found some Cuirassiers, genial fellows; but living *helios* in the burning sun. When I returned the Division had moved along the north bank of the Canal to Beuvry Station. The post picked us up, and in the joyous possession of two parcels and some letters I unpacked my kit. We all settled down on some moderately clean straw in the waiting-room of the station, and there we remained for three full weeks.

Men talk of the battle of Ypres[15] as the finest achievement of the British Army. There was one brigade there that had a past. It had fought at Mons and Le Cateau, and then plugged away cheerfully through the Retreat and the Advance. What was left of it had fought stiffly on the Aisne. Some hard marching, a train journey, more hard marching, and it was thrown into action at La Bassée. There it fought itself to a standstill. It was attacked and attacked until, shattered, it was driven back one wild night. It was rallied, and turning on the enemy held them. More hard marching—a couple of days' rest, and it staggered into action at Ypres, and somehow—no one knows how—it held its bit of line. A brigade called by the same name, consisting of the same regiments, commanded by the same general, but containing scarce a man of those who had come out in August, marched very proudly away from Ypres and went—not to rest—but to hold another bit of the line.

And this brigade was not the Guards Brigade. There were no picked men in the brigade. It contained just four ordinary regiments of the line—the Norfolks, the Bedfords, the Cheshires, and the Dorsets. What the 15th Brigade did, other brigades have done.

Now little has been heard of this fighting round La Bassée in October, so I wish I could tell you about it in more detail than I can. To my thinking it was the finest fighting I have seen.

You will understand, then, how difficult it is for me to describe the country round La Bassée. I might describe it as it appeared to me when first we arrived—sunny and joyous, with many little farms and thick hedges and rare factories—or as I saw it last, on a horrible yellowish evening, shattered and black and flooded and full of ghosts.

Now when first we arrived news filtered through to us that La Bassée was held only by a division of Jägers, plentifully supplied with artillery and machine guns. I believe this was the fact. The Jägers held on stubbornly until reinforcements came up.

15. The first—in October and November.

Instead of attacking we were hard pressed, and had more than we could do to prevent the Germans in their turn from breaking through. Indeed we had not a kick left in us when the Division was relieved.

At the beginning it looked so simple. The British Army was wheeling round on to the German right flank. We had the shortest distance to go, because we formed the extreme British right. On our left was the 3rd Division, and beyond the 3rd was the First Corps. On the left of the First the Third Corps was sweeping on to Armentières.

Then Antwerp fell suddenly. The First Corps was rushed up to help the Seventh Division which was trying to guard the right flank of the Belgians in retirement along the coast. Thus some sort of very weak line was formed from the sea to La Bassée. The Germans, reinforced by the men, and more particularly by the guns that the fall of Antwerp had let loose, attacked violently at Ypres and La Bassée. I do not say this is what really happened. I am trying to tell you what we thought was happening.

Think of us, then, in the heat of early October going into action on the left of the French, confident that we had just a little opposition to brush away in front of us before we concentrated in the square at La Bassée.

At first the 13th Brigade was put into position south of the canal, the 15th Brigade attacked from the canal to the La Bassée-Estaires road, and the 14th from the main road roughly to the Richebourgs. In the second stage the French extended their line to the Canal, and the 13th became a reserve brigade. In the third stage we had every man in the line—the 13th Brigade being split up between the 14th and 15th, and the French sent two battalions to the north bank of the canal.

The work of the despatch riders was of two kinds. Three-quarters of us rode between the divisional and the brigade headquarters. The rest were attached to the brigades, and either used for miscellaneous work or held in reserve so that communication might not be broken if the wires were cut or smashed by shells.

One motor-cyclist went out every day to Lieutenant Chapman, who was acting as liaison officer with the French. This job never fell to my lot, but I am told it was exciting enough. The French general was an intrepid old fellow, who believed that a general should be near his fighting men. So his headquarters were always being shelled. Then he would not retire, but preferred to descend into the cellar until the evil times were over.

The despatch rider with Chapman had his bellyful of shells. It was pleasant to sit calmly in a cellar and receive food at the hands of an accomplished *chef*, and in more peaceful times there was opportunity to study the idiosyncrasies of German gunners and the peculiar merits of the Soixante-Quinze. But when the shelling was hottest there was usually work for the despatch rider—and getting away from the unhealthy area before scooting down the Annequin road was a heart-thumping job.

French generals were always considerate and hospitable to us despatch riders. On our arrival at Béthune Huggie was sent off with a message to a certain French Corps Commander. The General received him with a proper French embrace, congratulated him on our English bravery, and set him down to some food and a glass of good wine.

It was at La Bassée that we had our first experience of utterly unrideable roads. North of the canal the roads were fair macadam in dry weather and to the south the main road Béthune-Beuvry-Annequin was of the finest *pavé*. Then it rained hard. First the roads became greasy beyond belief. Starting was perilous, and the slightest injudicious swerve meant a bad skid. Between Gorre and Festubert the road was vile. It went on raining, and the roads were thickly covered with glutinous mud. The front mud-guard of George's Douglas choked up with a lamentable frequency. The Blackburne alone, the finest and most even-running of all motor-cycles,[16] ran with unswerving regularity.

Finally, to our heartburning sorrow, there were nights on

16. This is not an unthinking advertisement. After despatch riding from August 16 to February 18 my judgment should be worth something. I am firmly convinced that if the Government could have provided all despatch riders with Blackburnes, the percentage—at all times small—of messages undelivered owing to mechanical breakdowns or the badness of the roads would have been reduced to zero. I have no interest in the Blackburne Company beyond a sincere admiration of the machine it produces.

which motor-cycling became impossible, and we stayed restlessly at home while men on the despised horse carried our despatches. This we could not allow for long. Soon we became so skilled that, if I remember correctly, it was only on half a dozen nights in all right through the winter that the horsemen were required.

It was at La Bassée too that we had our second casualty. A despatch rider whom we called "Moulders" came in one evening full of triumph. A bullet had just grazed his leg and the Government was compelled to provide him with a new puttee. We were jealous, and he was proud.

We slept in that room which was no room, the entrance-hall of Beuvry Station. It was small and crowded. The floor was covered with straw which we could not renew. After the first fortnight the population of this chamber increased rapidly; one or two of us spoke of himself hereafter in the plural. They gave far less trouble than we had expected, and, though always with some of us until the spring, suffered heavy casualties from the use of copious petrol and the baking of washed shirts in the village oven.

We had been given a cook of our own. He was a youth of dreamy habits and acquisitive tastes, but sometimes made a good stew. Each one of us thought he himself was talented beyond the ordinary, so the cook never wanted assistance—except perhaps in the preparing of breakfast. Food was good and plentiful, while the monotony of army rations was broken by supplies from home and from Béthune. George, thank heaven, was still with us.

Across the bridge was a shop where you could buy anything from a pair of boots to a kilo of *vermicelli*. Those of us who were not on duty would wander in about eleven in the morning, drink multitudinous bowls of coffee at two *sous* the bowl, and pass the time of day with some of the cyclists who were billeted in the big brewery. Just down the road was a tavern where infernal cognac could be got and occasionally good red wine.

Even when there was little to do, the station was not dull. French hussars, dainty men with thin and graceful horses, rode over the bridge and along the canal every morning. Cuirassiers would clatter and swagger by—and guns, both French and English. Behind the station much ammunition was stored, a source of keen pleasure if ever the Germans had attempted to shell the station. It was well within range. During the last week His Majesty's armoured train, *Jellicoe*, painted in wondrous colours, would rumble in and on towards La Bassée. The crew were full of Antwerp tales and late newspapers. The first time the train went into action it demolished a German battery, but afterwards it had little luck.

The corps was at Hinges. If work were slack and the Signal Sergeant were kind, he would give one of us a bunch of messages for the corps, with the hint that the return might be made at leisure. Between Hinges and Beuvry lay Béthune. Hinges deserves a word.

When first the corps came to Hinges, the inhabitants were exalted. The small boys came out in puttees and the women put ribbons in their hair. Now, if you pronounce Hinges in the French fashion, you give forth an exclamation of distressful pain. The name cannot be shouted from a motor-cycle. It has its difficulties even for the student of French. So we all called it, plainly and bluntly, Hinges, as though it were connected to a door. The inhabitants noticed this. Thinking that they and their forefathers had been wrong—for surely these fine men with red hats knew better than they—the English pronunciation spread. The village became 'Ingees, and now only some unfashionable dotards in Béthune preserve the tradition of the old pronunciation. It is not only Hinges that has been thus decently attired in British garb. Le Cateau is Lee Catòo. Boescheppe is Bo-peep. Ouderdon is Eiderdown.

Béthune was full of simple pleasures. First there were the public baths, cheap and good, and sundry coiffeurs who were much in demand, for they made you smell sweetly. Then there was a little blue and white café. The daughter of the house was well-favoured and played the piano with some skill. One of us spent all his spare time at this café in silent adoration—of the piano, for his French was exiguous in the extreme. There was a patisserie crammed full of the most delicious cream-cakes. The despatch rider who went to Hinges about 3.30 p.m. and did not return with cakes for tea, found life unpleasant. Near the station three damsels ruled a tavern. They were friendly and eager to teach us French. We might have left them with a sigh of regret if we had not once arrived as they were eating their midday meal.

At one time the Germans dropped a few shells into Béthune, but did little damage. Bombs fell too. One nearly ended the existence of "Sadders"—also known as "Boo." It dropped on the other side of the street; doing our despatch rider no damage, it slightly wounded Sergeant Croucher of the Cyclists in a portion of his body that made him swear when he was classed as a "sitting-up case."

Of all the towns behind the lines—Béthune, Estaires, Armentières, Bailleul, Poperinghe—Béthune is the pleasantest. The people are charming. There is nothing you cannot buy there. It is clean and well-ordered, and cheerful in the rain. I pray that Béthune may survive the war—that after peace has been declared and Berlin has been entered, I may spend a week there and much money to the profit of the people and the satisfaction of myself.

Now I will give some account of our adventures out with the brigades round La Bassée.

CHAPTER 9

Round La Bassée

It had been a melancholy day, full of rain and doubting news. Those of us who were not "out" were strolling up and down the platform arranging the order of cakes from home and trying to gather from the sound of the gunning and intermittent visits to the Signal Office what was happening.

Someone had been told that the old 15th was being hard pressed. Each of us regretted loudly that we had not been attached to it, though our hearts spoke differently. Despatch riders have muddled thoughts. There is a longing for the excitement of danger and a very earnest desire to keep away from it.

The C.O. walked on to the platform hurriedly, and in a minute or two I was off. It was lucky that the road was covered with unholy grease, that the light was bad and there was transport on the road—for it is not good for a despatch rider to think too much of what is before him. My instructions were to report to the general and make myself useful. I was also cheerfully informed that the H.Q. of the 15th were under a robust shell-fire. Little parties of sad-looking wounded that I passed, the noise of the guns, and the evil dusk heartened me.

I rode into Festubert, which was full of noise, and, very hastily dismounting, put my motor-cycle under the cover of an arch and reported to the general. He was sitting at a table in the stuffy room of a particularly dirty tavern. At the far end a fat and frightened woman was crooning to her child. Beside her sat a wrinkled, leathery old man with bandaged head. He had wandered into the street, and he had been cut about by shrapnel. The few wits he had ever possessed were gone, and he gave every few seconds little croaks of hate. Three telephone operators were working with strained faces at their highest speed. The windows had been smashed by shrapnel, and bits of glass and things crunched under foot. The room was full of noises—the crackle of the telephones, the crooning of the woman, the croak of the wounded old man, the clear and incisive tones of the general and his brigade-major, the rattle of not too distant rifles, the booming of guns and occasionally the terrific, overwhelming crash of a shell bursting in the village.

I was given a glass of wine. Cadell, the Brigade Signal Officer, and the Veterinary Officer, came up to me and talked cheerfully in whispered tones about our friends.

There was the sharp cry of shrapnel in the street and a sudden rattle against the whole house. The woman and child fled somewhere through a door, followed feebly by the old man. The brigade-major persuaded the general to work in some less unhealthy place. The telephone operators moved. A moment's delay as the general endeavoured to persuade the brigade-major to go first, and we found ourselves under a stalwart arch that led into the courtyard of the tavern. We lit pipes and cigarettes. The crashes of bursting shells grew more frequent, and the general remarked in a dry and injured tone—

"Their usual little evening shoot before putting up the shutters, I suppose."

But first the Germans "searched" the village. Now to search a village means to start at one end of the village and place shells at discreet intervals until the other end of the village is reached. It is an unpleasant process for those in the middle of the village, even though they be standing, as we were, in comparatively good shelter.

We heard the Germans start at the other end of the village street. The crashes came nearer and nearer, until a shell burst with a scream and a thunderous roar just on our right. We puffed away at our cigarettes for a second, and a certain despatch rider wished he were anywhere but in the cursed village of Festubert by Béthune. There was another scream and overwhelming relief.

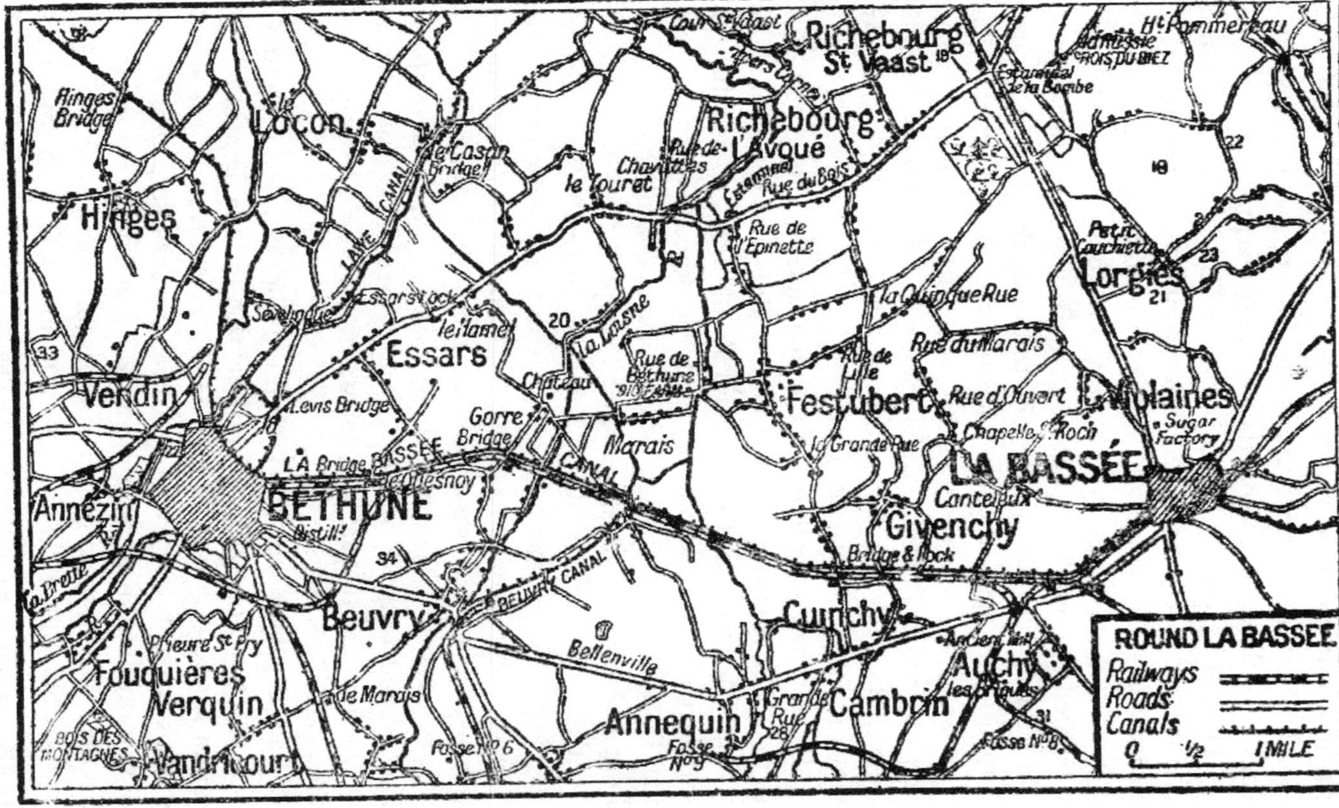
ROUND LA BASSEE
Railways
Roads
Canals
0
1/2
1 MILE
LA BASSÉE
BETHUNE
Richebourg St Vaast
Richebourg L'Avoué
Locon
Hinges
Hinges Bridge
Le Casan Bridge
Chavattes
le Touret
Rue du Bois
Rue de l'Epinette
la Quinque Rue
Rue du Marais
Rue de Lille
Festubert
Rue d'Ouvert
Chapelle St Roch
Violaines
Sugar Factory
Lorgies
Ht Pommereau
Estaminet de la Bombe
Essars
le Hamel
Essars Lock
La Loisne
Rue de Bethune
Chateau
Gorre Bridge
Marais
Levis Bridge
La Bridge
Distill.
Vendin
Annezin
La Brette
Beuvry
Beuvry Canal
Bellenville
Canteleux
Givenchy
Bridge & Lock
Cuinchy
Annequin
Grande Rue
Cambrin
Auchy
Ancient Mill
Fosse No. 6
Fosse No. 8
Prieure St Pry
Fouquières
Verquin
Vaudricourt
Bois des Montagnes
de Marais
la Grande Rue
La Bassée Canal
Canal

The next shell burst three houses away on our left. I knocked my pipe out and filled another.

The Germans finished their little evening shoot. We marched back very slowly in the darkness to 1910 Farm.

This farm was neither savoury nor safe. It was built round a courtyard which consisted of a gigantic hole crammed with manure in all the stages of unpleasant putrefaction. One side is a barn; two sides consist of stables, and the third is the house inhabited not only by us but by an incredibly filthy and stinking old woman who was continually troubling the general because some months ago a French cuirassier took one of her chickens. The day after we arrived at this farm I had few despatches to take, so I wrote to Robert. Here is some of the letter and bits of other letters I wrote during the following days. They will give you an idea of our state of mind:[17]

If you want something of the dramatic—I am writing in a farm under shrapnel fire, smoking a pipe that was broken by a shell. For true effect I suppose I should not tell you that the shrapnel is bursting about fifty yards the other side of the house, that I am in a room lying on the floor, and consequently that, so long as they go on firing shrapnel, I am perfectly safe.

It's the dismallest of places. Two miles farther back the heavies are banging away over our heads. There are a couple of batteries near the farm. Two miles along the road the four battalions of our brigade are holding on for dear life in their trenches.

The country is open plough, with little clumps of trees, sparse hedges, and isolated cottages giving a precarious cover. It's all very damp and miserable, for it was raining hard last night and the day before.

I am in a little bare room with the floor covered with straw. Two telegraph operators are making that infernal jerky clicking sound I have begun so to hate. Half a dozen men of the signal staff are lying about the floor looking at week-old papers. In the next room I can hear the general, seated at a table and intent on his map, talking to an officer that has just come from the firing line. Outside the window a gun is making a fiendish row, shak-

17. The letters were written on the 14th October *et seq.* The censor was kind.

ing the whole house. Occasionally there is a bit of a rattle—that's shrapnel bullets falling on the tiles of an outhouse.

If you came out you might probably find this exhilarating. I have just had a talk with our mutual friend Cadell, the Signal Officer of this brigade, and we have decided that we are fed up with it. For one thing—after two months' experience of shell fire the sound of a shell bursting within measurable distance makes you start and shiver for a moment—reflex action of the nerves. That is annoying. We both decided we would willingly change places with you and take a turn at defending your doubtless excellently executed trenches at Liberton.

The line to the ——[18] has just gone. It's almost certain death to relay it in the day-time. Cadell and his men are discussing the chances while somebody else has started a musical-box. A man has gone out; I wonder if he will come back. The rest of the men have gone to sleep again. That gun outside the window is getting on my nerves. Well, well!

The shrapnel fire appears to have stopped for the present. No, there's a couple together. If they fire over this farm I hope they don't send me back to D.H.Q.

Do you know what I long for more than anything else? A clean, unhurried breakfast with spotless napery and shining silver and porridge and kippers. I don't think these long, lazy after-breakfast hours at Oxford were wasted. They are a memory and a hope out here. The shrapnel is getting nearer and more frequent. We are all hoping it will kill some chickens in the courtyard. The laws against looting are so strict.

What an excellent musical-box, playing quite a good imitation of *Cavalleria Rusticana*. I guess we shall have to move soon. Too many shells. Too dark to write any more——

After all, quite the most important things out here are a fine meal and a good bath. If you consider the vast area of the war the facts that we have lost two guns or advanced five miles are of very little importance. War, making one realise the hopeless insignificance of the individual, creates in one such an im-

---

18. Dorsets, I think.

mense regard for self, that so long as one does well it matters little if four officers have been killed reconnoitring or some wounded have had to be left under an abandoned gun all night. I started with an immense interest in tactics. This has nearly all left me and I remain a more or less efficient despatch-carrying animal—a part of a machine realising the hopeless, enormous size of the machine.

The infantry officer after two months of modern war is a curious phenomenon.[19] He is probably one of three survivors of an original twenty-eight. He is not frightened of being killed; he has forgotten to think about it. But there is a sort of reflex fright. He becomes either cautious and liable to sudden panics, or very rash indeed, or absolutely mechanical in his actions. The first state means the approach of a nervous breakdown, the second a near death. There are very few, indeed, who retain a nervous balance and a calm judgment. And all have a harsh frightened voice. If you came suddenly out here, you would think they were all mortally afraid. But it is only giving orders for hours together under a heavy fire.

Battle noises are terrific. At the present moment a howitzer is going strong behind this, and the concussion is tremendous. The noise is like dropping a traction-engine on a huge tin tray. A shell passing away from you over your head is like the loud crackling of a newspaper close to your ear. It makes a sort of deep reverberating crackle in the air, gradually lessening, until there is a dull boom, and a mile or so away you see a thick little cloud of white smoke in the air or a pear-shaped cloud of grey-black smoke on the ground. Coming towards you a shell makes a cutting, swishing note, gradually getting higher and higher, louder and louder. There is a longer note one instant and then it ceases. Shrapnel bursting close to you has the worst sound.

It is almost funny in a village that is being shelled. Things simply disappear. You are standing in an archway a little back from the road—a shriek of shrapnel. The windows are broken and the tiles rush clattering into the street, while little bullets

19. I do not say this paragraph is true. It is what I thought on 15th October 1914. The weather was depressing.

and bits of shell jump like red-hot devils from side to side of the street, ricocheting until their force is spent. Or a deeper bang, a crash, and a whole house tumbles down.

Three-quarter hour later.—Curious life this. Just after I had finished the last sentence, I was called out to take a message to a battery telling them to shell a certain village. Here am I wandering out, taking orders for the complete destruction of a village and probably for the death of a couple of hundred men[20] without a thought, except that the roads are very greasy and that lunch time is near.

Again, yesterday, I put our Heavies in action, and in a quarter of an hour a fine old church, with what appeared from the distance a magnificent tower, was nothing but a grotesque heap of ruins. The Germans were loopholing it for defence.

Oh the waste, the utter damnable waste of everything out here—men, horses, buildings, cars, everything. Those who talk about war being a salutary discipline are those who remain at home. In a modern war there is little room for picturesque gallantry or picture-book heroism. We are all either animals or machines, with little gained except our emotions dulled and brutalised and nightmare flashes of scenes that cannot be written about because they are unbelievable. I wonder what difference you will find in us when we come home——

Do you know what a night scare is? In our last H.Q. we were all dining when suddenly there was a terrific outburst of rifle-fire from our lines. We went out into the road that passes the farm and stood there in the pitch darkness, wondering. The fire increased in intensity until every soldier within five miles seemed to be revelling in a lunatic succession of "mad minutes." Was it a heavy attack on our lines? Soon pom-poms joined in sharp, heavy taps—and machine guns. The lines to the battalions were at the moment working feebly, and what the operators could get through was scarcely intelligible. Ammunition limbers were hurried up, and I stood ready to dart anywhere. For twenty minutes the rifle-fire seemed to grow wilder and wilder. At last stretcher-bearers came in with a few wounded and reported

20. Optimist!

that we seemed to be holding our own. Satisfactory so far. Then there were great flashes of shrapnel over our lines; that comforted us, for if your troops are advancing you don't fire shrapnel over the enemy's lines. You never know how soon they may be yours. The firing soon died down until we heard nothing but little desultory bursts. Finally an orderly came—the Germans had half-heartedly charged our trenches but had been driven off with loss. We returned to the farm and found that in the few minutes we had been outside everything had been packed and half-frightened men were standing about for orders.

The explanation of it all came later and was simple enough. The French, without letting us know, had attacked the Germans on our right, and the Germans to keep us engaged had made a feint attack upon us. So we went back to dinner.

In modern war the infantryman hasn't much of a chance. Strategy nowadays consists in arranging for the mutual slaughter of infantry by the opposing guns, each general trusting that his guns will do the greater slaughter. And half gunnery is luck. The day before yesterday we had a little afternoon shoot at where we thought the German trenches might be. The Germans unaccountably retreated, and yesterday when we advanced we found the trenches crammed full of dead. By a combination of intelligent anticipation and good luck we had hit them exactly——

From these letters you will be able to gather what mood we were in and something of what the brigade despatch rider was doing. After the first day the Germans ceased shrapnelling the fields round the farm and left us nearly in peace. There I met Major Ballard, commanding the 15th Artillery Brigade, one of the finest officers of my acquaintance, and Captain Frost, the sole remaining officer of the Cheshires. He was charming to me; I was particularly grateful for the loan of a razor, for my own had disappeared and there were no despatch riders handy from whom I could borrow.

Talking of the Cheshires reminds me of a story illustrating the troubles of a brigadier. The general was dining calmly one night after having arranged an attack. All orders had been sent out. Everything was complete and ready. Suddenly there was a knock at the door and in walked Captain M——, who reported his arrival with 200 reinforcements for the Cheshires, a pleasant but irritating addition. The situation was further complicated by the general's discovery that M—— was senior to the officer then in command of the Cheshires. Poor M—— was not left long in command. A fortnight later the Germans broke through and over the Cheshires, and M—— died where a commanding officer should.

From 1910 Farm I had one good ride to the battalions, through Festubert and along to the Cuinchy bridge. For me it was interesting because it was one of the few times I had ridden just behind our trenches, which at the moment were just north of the road and were occupied by the Bedfords.

In a day or two we returned to Festubert, and Cadell gave me a shake-down on a mattress in his billet—gloriously comfortable. The room was a little draughty because the fuse of a shrapnel had gone right through the door and the fireplace opposite. Except for a peppering on the walls and some broken glass the house was not damaged; we almost laughed at the father and mother and daughter who, returning while we were there, wept because their home had been touched.

Orders came to attack. A beautiful plan was drawn up by which the battalions of the brigade were to finish their victorious career in the square of La Bassée.

In connection with this attack I was sent with a message for the Devons. It was the blackest of black nights and I was riding without a light. Twice I ran into the ditch, and finally I piled up myself and my bicycle on a heap of stones lying by the side of the road. I did not damage my bicycle. That was enough. I left it and walked.

When I got to Cuinchy bridge I found that the Devon headquarters had shifted. Beyond that the sentry knew nothing. Luckily I met a Devon officer who was bringing up ammunition. We searched the surrounding cottages for men with knowledge, and at last discovered that the Devons had moved farther along the canal in the direction of La Bassée. So we set out along the tow-path, past a house that was burning fiercely enough to make us conspicuous.

We felt our way about a quarter of a mile and stopped, because we were getting near the Germans. Indeed we could hear the rumble of their transport crossing the La Bassée bridge. We turned back, and a few yards nearer home some one coughed high up the bank on our right. We found the cough to be a sentry, and behind the sentry were the Devons.

The attack, as you know, was held up on the line Cuinchy-Givenchy-Violaines; we advanced our headquarters to a house just opposite the inn by which the road to Givenchy turns off. It was not very safe, but the only shell that burst anywhere near the house itself did nothing but wound a little girl in the leg.

On the previous day I had ridden to Violaines at dawn to draw a plan of the Cheshires' trenches for the general. I strolled out by the sugar factory, and had a good look at the red houses of La Bassée. Half an hour later a patrol went out to explore the sugar factory. They did not return. It seems that the factory was full of machine-guns. I had not been fired upon, because the Germans did not wish to give their position away sooner than was necessary.

A day or two later I had the happiness of avenging my potential death. First I took orders to a battery of 6-inch howitzers at the Rue de Marais to knock the factory to pieces, then I carried an observing officer to some haystacks by Violaines, from which he could get a good view of the factory. Finally I watched with supreme satisfaction the demolition of the factory, and with regretful joy the slaughter of the few Germans who, escaping, scuttled for shelter in some trenches just behind and on either side of the factory.

I left the 15th Brigade with regret, and the regret I felt would have been deeper if I had known what was going to happen to the brigade. I was given interesting work and made comfortable. No despatch rider could wish for more.

Not long after I had returned from the 15th Brigade, the Germans attacked and broke through. They had been heavily reinforced and our tentative offensive had been replaced by a stern and anxious defensive.

Now the Signal Office was established in the booking-office

of Beuvry Station. The little narrow room was packed full of operators and vibrant with buzz and click. The Signal Clerk sat at a table in a tiny room just off the booking-office. Orderlies would rush in with messages, and the Clerk would instantly decide whether to send them over the wire, by push-cyclist, or by despatch rider. Again, he dealt with all messages that came in over the wire. Copies of these messages were filed. This was our tape; from them we learned the news. We were not supposed to read them, but, as we often found that they contained information which was invaluable to despatch riders, we always looked through them and each passed on what he had found to the others. The Signal Clerk might not know where a certain unit was at a given moment. We knew, because we had put together information that we had gathered in the course of our rides and information which—though the Clerk might think it unimportant—supplemented or completed or verified what we had already obtained.

So the history of this partially successful attack was known to us. Every few minutes one of us went into the Signal Office and read the messages. When the order came for us to pack up, we had already made our preparations, for Divisional Headquarters, the brain controlling the actions of seventeen thousand men, must never be left in a position of danger. And wounded were pouring into the Field Ambulances.

The enemy had made a violent attack, preluded by heavy shelling, on the left of the 15th, and what I think was a holding attack on the right. Violaines had been stormed, and the Cheshires had been driven, still grimly fighting, to beyond the Rue de Marais. The Norfolks on their right and the K.O.S.B.'s on their left had been compelled to draw back their line with heavy loss, for their flanks had been uncovered by the retreat of the Cheshires.

The Germans stopped a moment to consolidate their gains. This gave us time to throw a couple of battalions against them. After desperate fighting Rue de Marais was retaken and some sort of line established. What was left of the Cheshires gradually rallied in Festubert.

This German success, together with a later success against the 3rd Division, that resulted in our evacuation of Neuve Chapelle, compelled us to withdraw and readjust our line. This second line was not so defensible as the first. Until we were relieved the Germans battered at it with gunnery all day and attacks all night. How we managed to hold it is utterly beyond my understanding. The men were dog-tired. Few of the old officers were left, and they were "done to the world." Never did the Fighting Fifth more deserve the name. It fought dully and instinctively, like a boxer who, after receiving heavy punishment, just manages to keep himself from being knocked out until the call of time.

Yet, when they had dragged themselves wearily and blindly out of the trenches, the fighting men of the Fighting Fifth were given but a day's rest or two before the 15th and two battalions of the 13th were sent to Hooge, and the remainder to hold sectors of the line farther south. Can you wonder that we despatch riders, in comparative safety behind the line, did all we could to help the most glorious and amazing infantry that the world has ever seen?[21] And when you praise the deeds of Ypres of the First Corps, who had experienced no La Bassée, spare a word for the men of the Fighting Fifth who thought they could fight no more and yet fought.

A few days after I had returned from the 15th Brigade I was sent out to the 14th. I found them at the Estaminet de l'Epinette on the Béthune-Richebourg road. Headquarters had been compelled to shift, hastily enough, from the Estaminet de La Bombe on the La Bassée-Estaires road. The estaminet had been shelled to destruction half an hour after the Brigade had moved. The Estaminet de l'Epinette was filthy and small. I slept in a stinking barn, half-full of dirty straw, and rose with the sun for the discomfort of it.

Opposite the estaminet a road goes to Festubert. At the corner there is a cluster of dishevelled houses. I sat at the door and wrote letters, and looked for what might come to pass. In the

---

21. After nine months at the Front—six and a half months as a despatch rider and two and a half months as a cyclist officer—I have decided that the English language has no superlative sufficient to describe our infantry.

early dawn the poplars alongside the highway were grey and dull. There was mist on the road; the leaves that lay thick were black. Then as the sun rose higher the poplars began to glisten and the mist rolled away, and the leaves were red and brown.

An old woman came up the road and prayed the sentry to let her pass. He could not understand her and called to me. She told me that her family were in the house at the corner fifty yards distant. I replied that she could not go to them—that they, if they were content not to return, might come to her. But the family would not leave their chickens, and cows, and corn. So the old woman, who was tired, sank down by the wayside and wept. This sorrow was no sorrow to the sorrow of the war. I left the old woman, the sentry, and the family, and went into a fine breakfast.

At this time there was much talk about spies. Our wires were often cut mysteriously. A sergeant had been set upon in a lane. The enemy were finding our guns with uncanny accuracy. All our movements seemed to be anticipated by the enemy. Taking for granted the extraordinary efficiency of the German Intelligence Corps, we were particularly nervous about spies when the Division was worn out, when things were not going well.

At the Estaminet de l'Epinette I heard a certain story, and hearing it set about to make a fool of myself. This is the story—I have never heard it substantiated, and give it as an illustration and not as fact.

There was once an artillery brigade billeted in a house two miles or so behind the lines. All the inhabitants of the house had fled, for the village had been heavily bombarded. Only a girl had had the courage to remain and do hostess to the English. She was so fresh and so charming, so clever in her cookery, and so modest in her demeanour that all the men of the brigade headquarters fell madly in love with her. They even quarrelled. Now this brigade was suffering much from espionage. The guns could not be moved without the Germans knowing their new position. No transport or ammunition limbers were safe from the enemy's guns. The brigade grew mightily indignant. The girl was told by her numerous sweethearts what was the matter. She was angry and sympathetic, and swore that through her the spy should be discovered. She swore the truth.

One night a certain lewd fellow of the baser sort pursued the girl with importunate pleadings. She confessed that she liked him, but not in that way. He left her and stood sullenly by the door. The girl took a pail and went down into the cellar to fetch up a little coal, telling the man with gentle mockery not to be so foolish. This angered him, and in a minute he had rushed after her into the cellar, snorting with disappointed passion. Of course he slipped on the stairs and fell with a crash. The girl screamed. The fellow, his knee bruised, tried to feel his way to the bottom of the stairs and touched a wire. Quickly running his hand along the wire he came to a telephone. The girl rushed to him, and, clasping his knees, offered him anything he might wish, if only he would say nothing. I think he must have hesitated for a moment, but he did not hesitate long. The girl was shot.

Full of this suspiciously melodramatic story I caught sight of a mysterious document fastened by nails to the house opposite the inn. It was covered with coloured signs which, whatever they were, certainly did not form letters or make sense in any way. I examined the document closely. One sign looked like an aeroplane, another like a house, a third like the rough drawing of a wood. I took it to a certain officer, who agreed with me that it appeared suspicious.

We carried it to the staff-captain, who pointed out very forcibly that it had been raining lately, that colour ran, that the signs left formed portions of letters. I demanded the owner of the house upon which the document had been posted. She was frightened and almost unintelligible, but supplied the missing fragments. The document was a crude election appeal. Being interpreted it read something like this—*support lefèvre. he is not a liar like dubois.*

Talking of spies, here is another story. It is true.

Certain wires were always being cut. At length a patrol was organised. While the operator was talking there was a little click and no further acknowledgment from the other end. The patrol started out and caught the man in the act of cutting a second wire. He said nothing.

He was brought before the Mayor. Evidence was briefly given of his guilt. He made no protest. It was stated that he had been born in the village. The Mayor turned to the man and said—

"You are a traitor. It is clear. Have you anything to say?"

The man stood white and straight. Then he bowed his head and made answer—

"Priez pour moi."

That was no defence. So they led him away.

The morning after I arrived at the 14th the Germans concentrated their fire on a large turnip-field and exhumed multitudinous turnips. No further damage was done, but the field was unhealthily near the Estaminet de l'Epinette. In the afternoon we moved our headquarters back a mile or so to a commodious and moderately clean farm with a forgettable name.

That evening two prisoners were brought in. They owned to eighteen, but did not look more than sixteen. The guard treated them with kindly contempt. We all sat round a makeshift table in the loft where we slept and told each other stories of fighting and love and fear, while the boys, squatting a little distance away, listened and looked at us in wonder. I came in from a ride about one in the morning and found those of the guard who were off duty and the two German boys sleeping side by side. Literally it was criminal negligence—someone ought to have been awake—but, when I saw one of the boys was clasping tightly a packet of Woodbines, I called it something else and went to sleep.

A day or two later I was relieved. On the following afternoon I was sent to Estaires to bring back some details about the Lahore Division which had just arrived on the line. I had, of course, seen Spahis and Turcos and Senegalese, but when riding through Lestrem I saw these Indian troops of ours the obvious thoughts tumbled over one another.

We despatch riders when first we met the Indians wondered how they would fight, how they would stand shell-fire and the climate—but chiefly we were filled with a sort of mental helplessness, riding among people when we could not even vaguely guess at what they were thinking. We could get no deeper than their appearance, dignified and clean and well-behaved.

In a few days I was back again at the 14th with Huggie. At dusk the General went out in his car to a certain village about three miles distant. Huggie went with him. An hour or so, and I was sent after him with a despatch. The road was almost unrideable with the worst sort of grease, the night was pitch-black and I was allowed no light. I slithered along at about six miles an hour, sticking out my legs for a permanent scaffolding. Many troops were lying down at the side of the road. An officer in a strained voice just warned me in time for me to avoid a deep shell-hole by inches. I delivered my despatch to the General. Outside the house I found two or three officers I knew. Two of them were young captains in command of battalions. Then I learned how hard put to it the Division was, and what the result is of nervous strain.

They had been fighting and fighting and fighting until their nerves were nothing but a jangling torture. And a counter-attack on Neuve Chapelle was being organised. Huggie told me afterwards that when the car had come along the road, all the men had jumped like startled animals and a few had turned to take cover. Why, if a child had met one of these men she would have taken him by the hand instinctively and told him not to be frightened, and defended him against anything that came. Yet it is said there are still those at home who will not stir to help. I do not see how this can possibly be true. It could not be true.

First we talked about the counter-attack, and which battalion would lead; then with a little manipulation we began to discuss musical comedy and the beauty of certain ladies. Again the talk would wander back to which battalion would lead.

I returned perilously with a despatch and left Huggie, to spend a disturbed night and experience those curious sensations which are caused by a shell bursting just across the road from the house.

The proposed attack was given up. If it had been carried out, those men would have fought as finely as they could. I do not know whether my admiration for the infantry or my hatred of war is the greater. I can express neither.

On the following day the Brigadier moved to a farm farther

north. It was the job of Huggie and myself to keep up communication between this farm and the brigade headquarters at the farm with the forgettable name. To ride four miles or so along country lanes from one farm to another does not sound particularly strenuous. It was. In the first place, the neighbourhood of the advanced farm was not healthy. The front gate was marked down by a sniper who fired not infrequently but a little high. Between the back gate and the main road was impassable mud. Again, the farm was only three-quarters of a mile behind our trenches, and "overs" went zipping through the farm buildings at all sorts of unexpected angles. There were German aeroplanes about, so we covered our stationary motor-cycles with straw.

Starting from brigade headquarters the despatch rider in half a mile was forced to pass the transport of a Field Ambulance. The men seemed to take a perverted delight in wandering aimlessly and deafly across the road, and in leaving anything on the road which could conceivably obstruct or annoy a motor-cyclist. Then came two and a half miles of winding country lanes. They were covered with grease. Every corner was blind. A particularly sharp turn to the right and the despatch rider rode a couple of hundred yards in front of a battery in action that the Germans were trying to find. A "hairpin" corner round a house followed. This he would take with remarkable skill and alacrity, because at this corner he was always sniped. The German's rifle was trained a trifle high. Coming into the final straight the despatch rider or one despatch rider rode for all he was worth. It was unpleasant to find new shell-holes just off the road each time you passed, or, as you came into the straight, to hear the shriek of shrapnel between you and the farm.

Huggie once arrived at the house of the "hairpin" bend simultaneously with a shell. The shell hit the house, the house did not hit Huggie, and the sniper forgot to snipe. So every one was pleased.

On my last journey I passed a bunch of wounded Sikhs. They were clinging to all their kit. One man was wounded in both his feet. He was being carried by two of his fellows. In his hands he clutched his boots.

The men did not know where to go or what to do. I could not make them understand, but I tried by gestures to show them where the ambulance was.

I saw two others—they were slightly wounded—talking fiercely together. At last they grasped their rifles firmly, and swinging round, limped back towards the line.

Huggie did most of the work that day, because during the greater part of the afternoon I was kept back at brigade headquarters.

In the evening I went out in the car to fetch the general. The car, which was old but stout, had been left behind by the Germans. The driver of it was a reservist who had been taken from his battalion. Day and night he tended and coaxed that car. He tied it together when it fell to pieces. At all times and in all places he drove that car, for he had no wish at all to return to the trenches.

On the following day Huggie and I were relieved. When we returned to our good old musty quarters at Beuvry men talked of a move. There were rumours of hard fighting in Ypres. Soon the Lahore Division came down towards our line and began to take over from us. The 14th Brigade was left to strengthen them. The 15th and 13th began to move north.

Early on the morning of October 29 we started, riding first along the canal by Béthune. As for Festubert, Givenchy, Violaines, Rue de Marais, Quinque Rue, and La Bassée, we never want to see them again.

CHAPTER 10

The Beginning of Winter

Before we came, Givenchy had been a little forgettable village upon a hill, Violaines a pleasant afternoon's walk for the working men in La Bassée, Festubert a gathering-place for the people who lived in the filthy farms around. We left Givenchy a jumble of shuttered houses and barricaded cellars. A few Germans were encamped upon the site of Violaines. The great clock of Festubert rusted quickly against a tavern wall. We hated La Bassée, because against La Bassée the Division had been broken. There are some square miles of earth that, like criminals, should not live.

Our orders were to reach Caestre not later than the Signal Company. Caestre is on the Cassel-Bailleul road, three miles north-east of Hazebrouck. These unattached rides across country are the most joyous things in the world for a despatch rider. There is never any need to hurry. You can take any road you will. You may choose your tavern for lunch with expert care. And when new ground is covered and new troops are seen, we capture sometimes those sharp delightful moments of thirsting interest that made the Retreat into an epic and the Advance a triumphant ballad.

N'Soon and myself left together. We skidded along the tow-path, passed the ever-cheerful cyclists, and, turning due north, ran into St Venant. The grease made us despatch riders look as if we were beginning to learn. I rode gently but surely down the side of the road into the gutter time after time. Pulling ourselves together, we managed to slide past some Indian transport without being kicked by the mules, who, whenever they smelt petrol, developed a strong offensive. Then we came upon a big gun, discreetly covered by tarpaulins. It was drawn by a monster traction-engine, and sad-faced men walked beside it. The steering of the traction-engine was a trifle loose, so N'Soon and I drew off into a field to let this solemn procession pass. One of the commands in the unpublished *Book of the Despatch Rider* is this—

> When you halt by the roadside to let guns pass or when you leave your motor-cycle unattended, first place it in a position of certain safety where it cannot possibly be knocked over, and then move it another fifty yards from the road. It is impossible for a gunner to see something by the roadside and not drive over it. Moreover, lorries when they skid, skid furiously.

Four miles short of Hazebrouck we caught up the rest. Proceeding in single file along the road, we endeavoured not to laugh, for—as one despatch rider said—it makes all the difference on grease which side of your mouth you put your pipe in. We reached Hazebrouck at midday. Spreading out—the manoeuvre had become a fine art—we searched the town. The Chapeau Rouge was well reported on, and there we lunched.

All those tourists who will deluge Flanders after the war should go to the Chapeau Rouge in Hazebrouck. There we had lentil soup and stewed kidneys, and roast veal with potatoes and leeks, fruit, cheese, and good red wine. So little was the charge that one of us offered to pay it all. There are other more fashionable hotels in Hazebrouck, but, trust the word of a despatch rider, the Chapeau Rouge beats them all.

Very content we rode on to Caestre, arriving there ten minutes before the advance-party of the Signal Company. Divisional Headquarters were established at the House of the Spy. The owner of the house had been well treated by the Germans when they had passed through a month before. Upon his door had been written this damning legend—*hier sind guetige leute*[22]—and, when on the departure of the Germans the house had been searched by an indignant populace, German newspapers had been discovered in his bedroom.

22. Here are kindly people

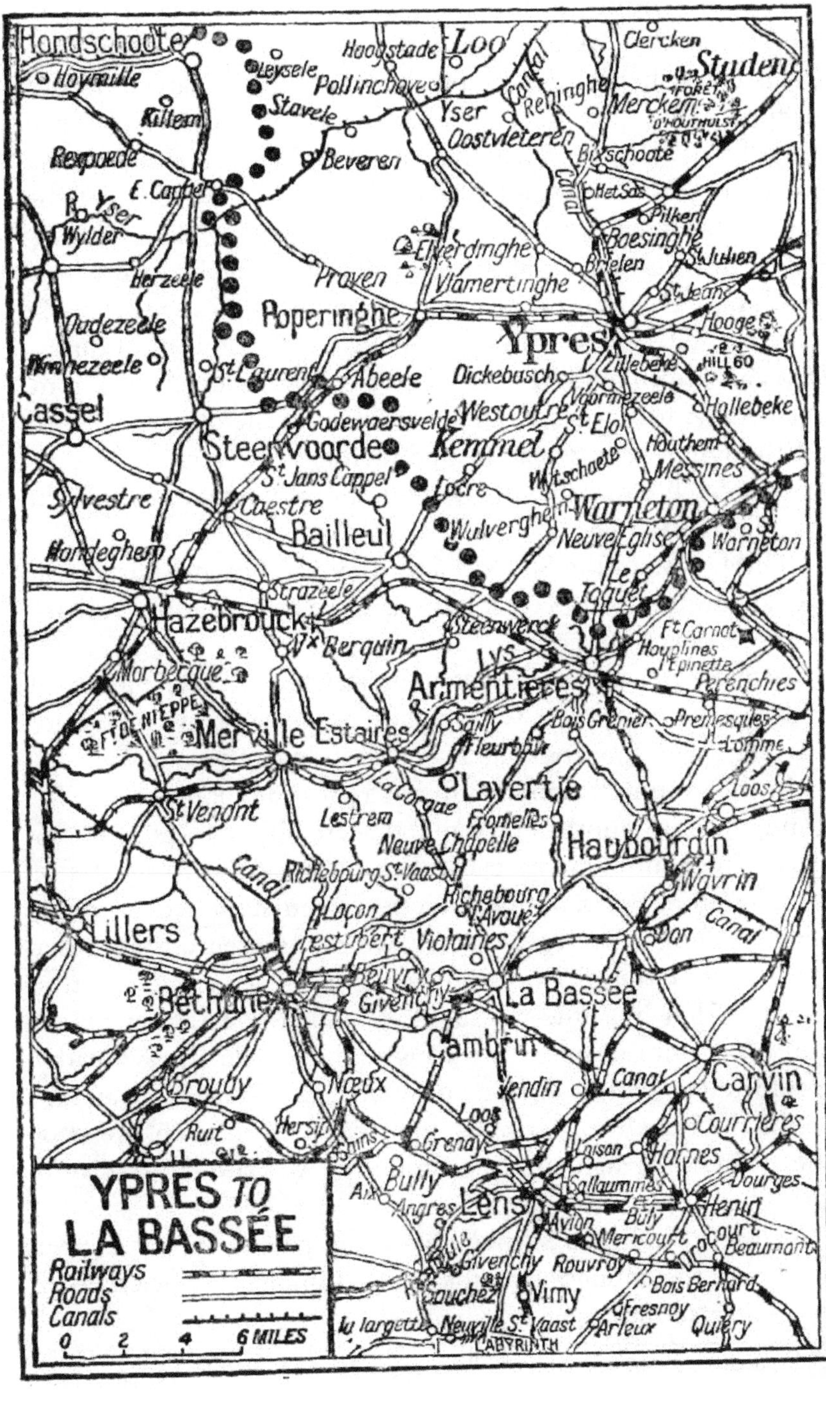

YPRES TO LA BASSÉE
Railways
Roads
Canals
0 2 4 6 MILES
Hondschoote
Hoymille
Killem
Rexpoede
Leysele
Stavele
Beveren
Hoogstade
Loo
Pollinchove
Yser
Oostvleteren
Canal
Reninghe
Clercken
Staden
Merckem
Bixschoote
Het Sas
Pilken
Boesinghe
St. Julien
St. Jean
Hooge
Hill 60
E. Cappel
Yser
Wylder
Herzeele
Oudezeele
Winnezeele
Cassel
Proven
Elverdinghe
Vlamertinghe
Brielen
Poperinghe
Ypres
Zillebeke
Abeele
Dickebusch
St. Laurent
Godewaersvelde
Westoutre
Voormezeele
St. Eloi
Hollebeke
Steenvoorde
Kemmel
Houthem
Messines
St. Jans Cappel
Locre
Wytschaete
Sylvestre
Caestre
Bailleul
Wulverghem
Warneton
Neuve Eglise
Hondeghem
Strazeele
Le Toquet
Hazebrouck
Steenwerck
Berquin
Lys
Ft. Carnot
Houplines
l'Epinette
Morbecque
Armentières
Perenchies
Ft. de Nieppe
Merville
Estaires
Sailly
Fleurbaix
Bois Grenier
Premesques
Lomme
Laventie
La Gorgue
Lestrem
St. Venant
Fromelles
Loos
Neuve Chapelle
Haubourdin
Canal
Richebourg St. Vaast
Richebourg l'Avoué
Wavrin
Locon
Lillers
Festubert
Violaines
Don
Canal
Beuvry
Béthune
Givenchy
La Bassée
Cambrin
Bruay
Noeux
Vendin
Canal
Carvin
Loos
Courrières
Ruit
Hersin
Grenay
Bully
Harnes
Sallaumines
Dourges
Aix
Angres
Lens
Avion
Billy
Henin
Souchez
Givenchy
Mericourt
Rouvroy
Beaumont
Vimy
Bois Berhard
Fresnoy
Neuville St. Vaast
Arleux
Quiery
Labyrinth

It is the custom of the Germans to spare certain houses in every village by chalking up some laudatory notice. We despatch riders had a theory that the inhabitants of these marked houses, far from being spies, were those against whom the Germans had some particular grievance. Imagine the wretched family doing everything in its power to avoid the effusive affection of the Teuton, breaking all its own crockery, and stealing all its own silver, defiling its beds and tearing its clothing. For the man whose goods have been spared by the German becomes an outcast. He lives in a state worse than death. He is hounded from his property, and driven across France with a character attached to him, like a kettle to a cat's tail. Genuine spies, on the other hand—so we thought—were worse treated than any and secretly recompensed. Such a man became a hero. All his neighbours brought their little offerings.

The House of the Spy had a fine garden, hot and buzzing in the languorous heat. We bathed ourselves in it. And the sanitary arrangements were good.

Grimers arrived lunchless an hour later. He had been promoted to drive the captured car. We took him to the tavern where beauty was allied with fine cooking. There he ate many omelettes.

In the evening he and I suffered a great disappointment. We wandered into another tavern and were about to ask for our usual Grenadine when we saw behind the bar two bottles of Worthington. For a moment we were too stupefied to speak. Then, pulling ourselves together, we stammered out an order for beer, but the girl only smiled. They were empty bottles, souvenirs left by some rascally A.S.C. for the eternal temptation of all who might pass through. The girl in her sympathy comforted us with songs, one of which, *Les Serments*, I translated for the benefit of Grimers, who knew no French. We sang cheerfully in French and English until it was time to return to our billet.

In the morning a German aeroplane passed over at a great height. All the youngsters in the village tumbled over each other for shelter, shouting—*Caput! Caput!*[23]

23. French, Flemish, and German slang expression. Done for!

Later in the day we advanced to Bailleul, where we learnt that the 1st Corps was fighting furiously to the north. The square was full of motor-buses and staff-officers. They were the first of our own motor-buses we had seen out in Flanders. They cheered us greatly, and after some drinks we sat in one and tried to learn from the map something of the new country in which we were to ride. We rejoiced that we had come once again upon a Belgian sheet, because the old French map we had used, however admirable it might have been for brigadiers and suchlike people, was extremely unsuited to a despatch rider's work.

Infantry were pouring through, the stern remnants of fine battalions. Ever since the night after Le Cateau infantry in column of route have fascinated us, for a regiment on the march bares its character to the world.

First there were our brigades marching up to Mons, stalwart and cheering. After Le Cateau there were practically no battalions, just a crowd of men and transport pouring along the road to Paris. I watched the column pass for an hour, and in it there was no organised unit larger than a platoon, and only one platoon. How it happened I do not know, but, when we turned on the Germans, battalions, brigades, divisions, corps had been remade. The battalions were pitifully small. Many a time we who were watching said to one another: Surely that's not the end of the K.O.Y.L.I., or the Bedfords, or whatever regiment it might be!

A battalion going into action has some men singing, some smiling vaguely to themselves, some looking raptly straight ahead, and some talking quickly as if they must never stop.

A battalion that has come many miles is nearly silent. The strong men stride tirelessly without a word. Little weak men, marching on their nerves, hobble restlessly along. The men with bad feet limp and curse, wilting under the burden of their kit, and behind all come those who have fallen out by the way—men dragging themselves along behind a wagon, white-faced men with uneasy smiles on top of the wagons. A little farther back those who are trying to catch up: these are tragic figures, breaking into breathless little runs, but with a fine wavering attempt at striding out, as though they might be connecting files, when they march through a town or past an officer of high rank.

A battalion that has just come out of action I cannot describe to you in these letters, but let me tell you now about Princess Pat's. I ran into them just as they were coming into Bailleul for the first time and were hearing the sound of the guns. They were the finest lot of men I have ever seen on the march. Gusts of great laughter were running through them. In the eyes of one or two were tears. And I told those civilians I passed that the Canadians, the fiercest of all soldiers, were come. Bailleul looked on them with more fright than admiration. The women whispered fearfully to each other—*"Les Canadiens, les Canadiens!*

We despatch riders were given a large room in the house where the Divisional Staff was billeted. It had tables, chairs, a fireplace and gas that actually lit; so we were more comfortable than ever we had been before—that is, all except N'Soon, who had by this time discovered that continual riding on bad roads is apt to produce a fundamental soreness. N'Soon hung on nobly, but was at last sent away with blood-poisoning. Never getting home, he spent many weary months in peculiar convalescent camps, and did not join up again until the end of January. Moral—before going sick or getting wounded become an officer and a gentleman.

The day after we arrived I was once more back in Belgium with a message to the C.R.A.[24] at Neuve Eglise. I had last been in Belgium on August 23, the day we left Dour.

The general might have been posing for a war artist. He was seated at a table in the middle of a field, his staff-captain with him. The ground sloped away to a wooded valley in which two or three batteries, carefully concealed, were blazing away. To the north shrapnel was bursting over Kemmel. In front the Messines ridge was almost hidden with the smoke of our shells. I felt that each point of interest ought to have been labelled in Mr Frederic Villiers' handwriting—*German shrapnel bursting over Kemmel—our guns—this is a dead horse.*

24. An abbreviation for the general in command of the Divisional Artillery.

I first saw Ypres on the 6th November. I was sent off with a bundle of routine matter to the 1st Corps, then at Brielen, a couple of miles N.W. of Ypres. It was a nightmare ride. The road was *pavé* in the centre—villainous *pavé*. At the side of it were glutinous morasses about six feet in width, and sixteen inches deep. I started off with two 2nd Corps motor-cyclists. There was an almost continuous line of transport on the road—motor-lorries that did not dare deviate an inch from the centre of the road for fear of slipping into the mire, motor ambulances, every kind of transport, and some infantry battalions. After following a column of motor-lorries a couple of miles—we stuck twice in trying to get past the rearmost lorry—we tried the road by Dranoutre and Locre. But these country lanes were worse of surface than the main road—greasy *pavé* is better that greasy rocks—and they were filled with odd detachments of French artillery. The two 2nd Corps motor-cyclists turned back. I crawled on at the risk of smashing my motor-cycle and myself, now skidding perilously between wagons, now clogging up, now taking to the fields, now driving frightened pedestrians off what the Belgians alone would call a footpath. I skidded into a subaltern, and each of us turned to curse, when—it was Gibson, a junior "Greats" don at Balliol, and the finest of fellows.

Beyond Dickebusch French artillery were in action on the road. The houses just outside Ypres had been pelted with shrapnel but not destroyed. Just by the station, which had not then been badly knocked about, I learnt where to go. Ypres was the first half-evacuated town I had entered. It was like motor-cycling into a village from Oxford very early on a Sunday morning. Half an hour later I saw the towers of the city rising above a bank of mist which had begun to settle on the ground: then out rose great clouds of black smoke.

I came back by Poperinghe to avoid the grease and crowding of the direct road, and there being no hurry I stopped at an inn for a beefsteak. The landlord's daughter talked of the many difficulties before us, and doubted of our success. I said, grandiloquently enough, that no victory was worth winning unless there were difficulties. At which she smiled and remarked, laughing—

"There are no roses without thorns."

She asked me how long the war would last. I replied that the good God alone knew. She shook her head—

"How can the good God look down without a tear on the miseries of his people? Are not the flower of the young cut off in the spring of their youth?"

Then she pointed to the church across the way, and said humbly—"On a *beaucoup prié.*"

She was of the true Flemish type, broad and big-breasted, but with a slight stoop, thick hips, dark and fresh-coloured, with large black eyes set too closely. Like all the Flemings, she spoke French slowly and distinctly, with an accent like the German. She was easy to understand.

I stopped too long at Poperinghe, for it was dark and very misty on the road. Beyond Boescheppe—I was out of my way—the mist became a fog. Once I had to take to the ditch when some cuirassiers galloped out of the fog straight at me. It was all four French soldiers could do to get my motor-cycle out. Another time I stuck endeavouring to avoid some lorries. It is a diabolical joke of the Comic Imps to put fog upon a greasy road for the confusion of a despatch rider.

On the next day I was sent out to the 14th Brigade at the Rue de Paradis near Laventie. You will remember that the 14th Brigade had been left to strengthen the Indian Corps when the 2nd Corps had moved north. I arrived at Rue de Paradis just as the Brigade Headquarters were coming into the village. So, while everybody else was fixing wires and generally making themselves useful, I rushed upstairs and seized a mattress and put it into a dark little dressing-room with hot and cold water, a mirror and a wardrobe. Then I locked the door. There I slept, washed, and dressed in delicious luxury.

The brigade gave another despatch rider and myself, who were attached, very little to do beyond an occasional forty-mile run to D.H.Q. and back over dull roads. The signal office was established in a large room on the side of the house nearest to the Germans. It was constructed almost entirely of glass. Upon this the men commented with a grave fluency. The windows rattled with shrapnel bursting 600 yards away. The house was jarred through and through by the concussion of a heavy battery firing over our heads. The room was like a toy-shop with a lot of small children sounding all the musical toys. The vibrators and the buzzers were like hoarse toy trumpets.

Our only excitement was the nightly rumour that the General was going to move nearer the trenches, that one of us would accompany him—I knew what that meant on greasy misty roads.

After I had left, the Germans by chance or design made better practice. A shell burst in the garden and shattered all the windows of the room. The Staff took refuge in dug-outs that had been made in case of need. Tommy, then attached, took refuge in the cellar. According to his own account, when he woke up in the morning he was floating. The house had some corners taken off it and all the glass was shattered, but no one was hurt.

When I returned to Bailleul, Divisional Headquarters were about to move.

A puncture kept me at Bailleul after the others had gone on to Locre. Grimers stood by to help. We lunched well, and buying some supplies started off along the Ypres road. By this time our kit had accumulated. It is difficult enough to pass lorries on a greasy road at any time. With an immense weight on the carrier it is almost impossible. So we determined to go by Dranoutre. An unfortunate bump dispersed my blankets and my groundsheet in the mud. Grimers said my language might have dried them. Finally, that other despatch rider arrived swathed about with some filthy, grey, forlorn indescribables.

We were quartered in a large schoolroom belonging to the Convent. We had plenty of space and a table to feed at. Fresh milk and butter we could buy from the nuns, while a market-gardener just across the road supplied us with a sack of miscellaneous vegetables—potatoes, carrots, turnips, onions, leeks—for practically nothing. We lived gloriously. There was just enough work to make us feel we really were doing something, and not enough to make us wish we were on the Staff. Bridge we played every hour of the day, and "Pollers," our sergeant, would occasionally try a little flutter in Dominoes and Patience.

At Bailleul the Skipper had suggested our learning to manage the unmechanical horse. The suggestion became an order. We were bumped round unmercifully at first, until many of us were so sore that the touch of a motor-cycle saddle on *pavé* was like hot-iron to a tender skin. Then we were handed over to a friendly sergeant, who believed in more gentlemanly methods, and at Locre we had great rides—though Pollers, who was gently unhorsed, is still firmly convinced that wind-mills form the finest deterrent to cavalry.

In an unlucky moment two of us had suggested that we should like to learn signaller's work, so we fell upon evil days. First we went out for cable-drill. Sounds simple? But it is more arduous and dangerous than any despatch riding. If you "pay out" too quickly, you get tangled up in the wire and go with it nicely over the drum. If you pay out too slowly, you strangle the man on the horse behind you. The worst torture in the world is paying out at the fast trot over cobbles. First you can't hold on, and if you can you can't pay out regularly.

Cable-drill is simply nothing compared to the real laying of cable. We did it twice—once in rain and once in snow. The rainy day I paid out, I was never more miserable in my life than I was after two miles. Only hot coffee and singing good songs past cheery *Piou-pious* brought me home. The snowy day I ran with ladders, and, perched on the topmost rung, endeavoured to pass the wire round a buxom tree-trunk. Then, when it was round, it would always go slack before I could get it tied up tightly.

It sounds so easy, laying a wire. But I swear it is the most wearying business in the world—punching holes in the ground with a 16-lb. hammer, running up poles that won't go straight, unhooking wire that has caught in a branch or in the eaves of a house, taking the strain of a cable to prevent man and ladder and wire coming on top of you, when the man who pays out has forgotten to pay. Have a thought for the wretched fellows who are getting out a wire on a dark and snowy night, troubled perhaps by persistent snipers and frequent shells! Shed a tear for the miserable linesman sent out to find where the line is broken or defective....

When there was no chance of "a run" we would go for walks towards Kemmel. At the time the Germans were shelling the hill, but occasionally they would break off, and then we would unofficially go up and see what had happened.

Now Mont Kemmel is nearly covered with trees. I have never been in a wood under shell fire, and I do not wish to be. Where the Germans had heavily shelled Kemmel there were great holes, trees thrown about and riven and scarred and crushed—a terrific immensity of blasphemous effort. It was as if some great beast, wounded mortally, had plunged into a forest, lashing and biting and tearing in his agony until he died.

On one side of the hill was a little crazy cottage which had marvellously escaped. Three shells had fallen within ten yards of it. Two had not burst, and the other, shrapnel, had exploded in the earth. The owner came out, a trifling, wizened old man in the usual Belgian cap and blue overalls. We had a talk, using the *lingua franca* of French, English with a Scottish accent, German, and the few words of Dutch I could remember.

We dug up for him a large bit of the casing of the shrapnel. He examined it fearfully. It was an 11-inch shell, I think, nearly as big as his wee grotesque self. Then he made a noise, which we took to be a laugh, and told us that he had been very frightened in his little house (*häusling*), and his cat, an immense white Tom, had been more frightened still. But he knew the Germans could not hit him. Thousands and thousands of Germans had gone by, and a little after the last German came the English. *"Les Anglais sont bons."*

This he said with an air of finality. It is a full-blooded judgment which, though it sounds a trifle exiguous to describe our manifold heroic efforts, is a sort of perpetual epithet. The children use it confidingly when they run to our men in the cafés. The peasants use it as a parenthetical verdict whenever they mention our name. The French fellows use it, and I have heard a German prisoner say the same.

A few days later those who lived on Kemmel were "evacuated." They were rounded up into the Convent yard, men and women and children, with their hens and pigs. At first they were angry and sorrowful; but nobody, not even the most indignant refugee, could resist our military policemen, and in three-quarters of an hour they all trudged off, cheerfully enough, along the road to Bailleul.

The wee grotesque man and his immense white cat were not with them. Perhaps they still live on Kemmel. Some time I shall go and see....

If we did not play Bridge after our walks, we would look in at the theatre or stroll across to dinner and Bridge with Gibson and his brother officers of the K.O.S.B., then billeted at Locre.

Not all convents have theatres: this was a special convent. The Signal Company slept in the theatre, and of an evening all the kit would be moved aside. One of the military policemen could play anything; so we danced and sang until the lights went out. The star performer was "Spot," the servant of an A.D.C.

"Spot" was a little man with a cheerful squint. He knew everything that had ever been recited, and his knowledge of the more ungodly songs was immense. He would start off with an imitation of Mr H.B. Irving, and a very good imitation it would be—with soft music. He would leave the Signallers thrilled and silent. The lights flashed up, and "Spot" darted off on some catchy doggerel of an almost talented obscenity. In private life Spot was the best company imaginable. He could not talk for a minute without throwing in a bit of a recitation and striking an attitude. I have only known him serious on two subjects—his master and Posh. He would pour out with the keenest delight little stories of how his master endeavoured to correct his servant's accent. There was a famous story of "a n'orse"—but that is untellable.

Posh may be defined, very roughly, as a useless striving after gentlemanly culture. Sometimes a chauffeur or an H.Q. clerk would endeavour to speak very correct English in front of Spot.

"'E was poshy, my dear boy, positively poshy. 'E made me shiver until I cried. 'Smith, old man,' I said to 'im, 'you can't do it. You're not born to it nor bred to it. Those that try is just demeaning themselves. Posh, my dear boy, pure posh.'"

And Spot would give a cruel imitation of the wretched Smith's mincing English. The punishment was the more bitter, because all the world knew that Spot could speak the King's English as well as anybody if only he chose. To the poshy alone was Spot unkind. He was a generous, warm-hearted little man, with real wisdom and a fine appreciation of men and things.... There were other performers of the usual type, young men who sang about the love-light in her eyes, older men with crude songs, and a Scotsman with an expressionless face, who mumbled about we could never discover what.

The audience was usually strengthened by some half-witted girls that the Convent educated, and two angelic nuns. Luckily for them, they only understood a slow and grammatical English, and listened to crude songs and sentimental songs with the same expression of maternal content.

Our work at Locre was not confined to riding and cable-laying. The 15th Brigade and two battalions of the 13th were fighting crazily at Ypres, the 14th had come up to Dranoutre, and the remaining two battalions of the 13th were at Neuve Eglise.

I had two more runs to the Ypres district before we left Locre. On the first the road was tolerable to Ypres, though near the city I was nearly blown off my bicycle by the fire of a concealed battery of 75's. The houses at the point where the Rue de Lille enters the Square had been blown to bits. The Cloth Hall had barely been touched. In its glorious dignity it was beautiful.

Beyond Ypres, on the Hooge Road, I first experienced the extreme neighbourhood of a "J.J." It fell about 90 yards in front of me and 20 yards off the road. It makes a curiously low droning sound as it falls, like the groan of a vastly sorrowful soul in hell—so I wrote at the time: then there's a gigantic rushing plunk and overwhelming crash as if all the houses in the world were falling.

On the way back the road, which had been fairly greasy, became practically impassable. I struggled on until my lamp failed (sheer carelessness—I ought to have seen to it before starting), and a gale arose which blew me all over the road. So I left my motor-bicycle safely behind a cottage, and started tramping back to H.Q. by the light of my pocket flash-lamp. It was a pitch-black night. I was furiously hungry, and stopped at the first inn and gorged coffee with rum, and a large sandwich of bread and butter and fat bacon. I had barely started again—it had begun to pour—when a car came along with a French staff-officer inside. I stopped it, saying in hurried and weighty tones that I was carrying an important despatch (I had nothing on me, I am afraid, but a trifling bunch of receipts), and the rest of the way I travelled lapped luxuriously in soft furs.

The second time I rode along a frozen road between white fields. All the shells sounded alarmingly near. The noise in Ypres was terrific. At my destination I came across some prisoners of the Prussian Guard, fierce and enormous men, nearly all with reddish hair, very sullen and rude.

From accounts that have been published of the first battle of Ypres, it might be inferred that the British Army knew it was on the point of being annihilated. A despatch rider, though of course he does not know very much of the real meaning of the military situation, has unequalled opportunities for finding out the opinions and spirit of the men. Now one of us went to Ypres every day and stopped for a few minutes to discuss the state of affairs with other despatch riders and with signal-sergeants. Right through the battle we were confident; in fact the idea that the line might be broken never entered our heads. We were suffering very heavily. That we knew. Nothing like the shell fire had ever been heard before. Nobody realised how serious the situation must have been until the accounts were published.

Huggie has a perfect mania for getting frightened; so one day, instead of leaving the routine matter that he carried at a place whence it might be forwarded at leisure, he rode along the Menin road to the Chateau at Hooge, the headquarters of the 15th Brigade. He came back quietly happy, telling us that he had had a good time, though the noise had been a little overwhelming. We learned afterwards that the enemy had been registering very accurately upon the Hooge road.

So the time passed without any excitement until November 23, when first we caught hold of a definite rumour that we should be granted leave. We existed in restless excitement until the 27th. On that great day we were told that we should be allowed a week's leave. We solemnly drew lots, and I drew the second batch.

We left the Convent at Locre in a dream, and took up quarters at St Jans Cappel, two miles west of Bailleul. We hardly noticed that our billet was confined and uncomfortable. Certainly we never realised that we should stop there until the spring. The first batch went off hilariously, and with slow pace our day drew nearer and nearer.

You may think it a little needless of me to write about my leave, if you do not remember that we despatch riders of the Fifth Division enlisted on or about August 6. Few then realised that England had gone to war. Nobody realised what sort of a war the war was going to be. When we returned in the beginning of December we were Martians. For three months we had been vividly soldiers. We had been fighting not in a savage country, but in a civilised country burnt by war; and it was because of this that the sights of war had struck us so fiercely that when we came back our voyage in the good ship *Archimedes* seemed so many years distant. Besides, if I were not to tell you of my leave it would make such a gap in my memories that I should scarcely know how to continue my tale....

The week dragged more slowly than I can describe. Shorthanded, we had plenty of work to do, but it was all routine work, which gave us too much time to think. There was also a crazy doubt of the others' return. They were due back a few hours before we started. If they fell ill or missed the boat...! And the fools were motor-cycling to and from Boulogne!

On the great night we prepared some food for them, and having packed our kits, tried to sleep. As the hour drew near we listened excitedly for the noise of their engines. Several false alarms disturbed us: first, a despatch rider from the Third Division, and then another from the Corps. At last we heard the purr of three engines together, and then a moment later the faint rustle of others in the distance. We recognised the engines and jumped up. All the birds came home save one. George had never quite recovered from his riding exercises.

Slight blood poisoning had set in. His leave had been extended at home. So poor "Tommy," who had joined us at Beuvry, was compelled to remain behind.

Violent question and answer for an hour, then we piled ourselves on our light lorry. Singing like angels we rattled into Bailleul. Just opposite Corps Headquarters, our old billet, we found a little crowd waiting. None of us could talk much for the excitement. We just wandered about greeting friends. I met again that stoutest of warriors, Mr Potter of the 15th Artillery Brigade, a friend of Festubert days. Then a battalion of French infantry passed through, gallant and cheerful men. At last the old dark-green buses rolled up, and about three in the morning we pounded off at a good fifteen miles an hour along the Cassel road.

Two of us sat on top, for it was a gorgeous night. We rattled over the *pavé* alongside multitudinous transport sleeping at the side of the road—through Metern, through Caestre of pleasant memories, and south to Hazebrouck. Our driver was a man of mark, a racing motorist in times of peace. He left the other buses and swung along rapidly by himself. He slowed down for nothing. Just before Hazebrouck we caught up a French convoy. I do not quite know what happened. The Frenchmen took cover in one ditch. We swayed past, half in the other, at a good round pace. Wagons seemed to disappear under our wheels, and frightened horses plunged violently across the road. But we passed them without a scratch—to be stopped by the level-crossing at Hazebrouck. There we filled up with coffee and cognac, while the driver told us of his adventures in Antwerp.

We rumbled out of Hazebrouck towards St Omer. It was a clear dawn in splashes of pure colour. All the villages were peaceful, untouched by war. When we came to St Omer it was quite light. All the soldiers in the town looked amateurish. We could not make out what was the matter with them, until somebody noticed that their buttons shone. We drew up in the square, the happiest crew imaginable, but with a dignity such as befitted chosen N.C.O.'s and officers.

That was the first time I saw St Omer. When last I came to it I saw little, because I arrived in a motor-ambulance and left in a hospital-train.

The top of the bus was crowded, and we talked "shop" together. Sixth Division's having a pretty cushy time, what?—So you were at Mons! (in a tone of respect)—I don't mind their shells, and I don't mind their machine-guns, but their *Minenwerfer* are the frozen limit!—I suppose there's no chance of our missing the boat. Yes, it was a pretty fair scrap—Smith? He's gone. Silly fool, wanted to have a look round—Full of buck? Rather! Yes, heard there's a pretty good show on at the Frivolity—Beastly cold on top of this old wheezer.

It was, but none of us cared a scrap. We looked at the sign-posts that showed the distance to Boulogne, and then pretended that we had not seen them. Lurching and skidding and toiling we came to the top of the hill above Boulogne. With screaming brakes we rattled down to the harbour. That old sinner, Sergeant Maguire, who was in charge of us corporals, made all arrangements efficiently. We embarked, and after a year of Sundays cast off.

There was a certain swell on, and Mr Potter, the bravest of men, grew greener and greener. My faith in mankind went.

We saw a dark line on the horizon.

"By Jove, there's England!" We all produced our field-glasses and looked through them very carefully for quite a long time.

"So it is. Funny old country"—a pause—"Makes one feel quite sentimental, just like the books. That's what we're fighting for, I suppose. Wouldn't fight for dirty old Dover! Wonder if they still charge you a penny for each sardine. I suppose we'll have to draw the blinds all the way up to London. Not a safe country by any means, far rather stop in the jolly old trenches."

"You'll get the white feather, old man."

"No pretty young thing would give it you. Why, you wouldn't look medically fit in mufti!"

"Fancy seeing a woman who isn't dirty and can talk one's own lingo!"

So we came to Folkestone, and all the people on the pier smiled at us. We scuttled ashore and shook ourselves for delight.

There was a policeman, a postman. Who are these fussy fellows with badges on their arms? Special constables, of course!

Spurning cigarettes and Bovril we rushed to the bar. We all noticed the cleanness of the barmaid, her beauty, the neatness of her dress, her cultivated talk. We almost squabbled about what drinks we should have first. Finally, we divided into parties—the Beers and the Whisky-and-Sodas. Then there were English papers to buy, and, of course, we must have a luncheon-basket....

The smell of the musty S.-E. & C.R. compartment was the scent of eastern roses. We sniffed with joy in the tunnels. We read all the notices with care. Nearing London we became silent. Quite disregarding the order to lower the blinds, we gazed from the bridge at a darkened London and the searchlight beams. Feverishly we packed our kit and stood up in the carriage. We jerked into the flare of Victoria. Dazzled and confused, we looked at the dense crowd of beaming, anxious people. There was a tug at my elbow, and a triumphant voice shouted—

"I've found him! Here he is! There's your Mother." ...

This strange familiar country seemed to us clean, careless, and full of men. The streets were clean; the men and women were clean. Out in Flanders a little grime came as a matter of course. One's uniform was dirty. Well, it had seen service. There was no need to be particular about the set of the tunic and the exact way accoutrements should be put on. But here the few men in khaki sprinkled about the streets had their buttons cleaned and not a thing was out of place. We wondered which of them belonged to the New Armies. The women, too, were clean and beautiful. This sounds perhaps to you a foolish thing to say, but it is true. The Flemish woman is not so clean as she is painted, and as for women dressed with any attempt at fashionable display—we had seen none since August. Nadine at Dour had been neat; Hélène at Carlepont had been companionable; the pretty *midinette* at Maast had been friendly and not over-dirty. For a day or two after I returned to my own country I could not imagine how anybody ever could leave it.

And all the people were free from care. However cheerful those brave but irritating folk who live behind the line may be, they have always shadows in their eyes. We had never been to a village through which the Germans had not passed. Portly and hilarious the Teuton may have shown himself—kindly and well-behaved he undoubtedly was in many places—there came with him a terror which stayed after he had gone, just as a mist sways above the ground after the night has flown.

At first we thought that no one at home cared about the war—then we realised it was impossible for anybody to care about the war who had not seen war. People might be intensely interested in the course of operations. They might burn for their country's success, and flame out against those who threatened her. They might suffer torments of anxiety for a brother in danger, or the tortures of grief for a brother who had died. The FACT of war, the terror and the shame, the bestiality and the awful horror, the pity and the disgust—they could never *know* war. So we thought them careless....

Again, though we had been told very many had enlisted, the streets seemed ludicrously full of men. In the streets of Flanders there are women and children and old men and others. These others would give all that they had to put on uniform and march gravely or gaily to the trenches. In Flanders a man who is fit and wears no uniform is instantly suspected of espionage. I am grinding no axe. I am advocating nothing or attacking nothing. I am merely stating as a fact that, suspicious and contemptuous as we had been in Flanders of every able-bodied man who was not helping to defend his country, it seemed grotesque to us to find so many civilian men in the streets of the country to which we had returned.

Of the heavenly quietness and decency of life, of late breakfasts and later dinners, there is no need to tell, but even before the week was up unrest troubled us. The Division might go violently into action. The Germans might break through. The "old Div." would be wanting us, and we who felt towards the Division as others feel towards their Regiments were eager to get back....

On the boat I met Gibson. At Boulogne we clambered into the same bus and passed the time in sipping old rum, eating chocolate biscuits, reading the second volume of 'Sinister Street,' and sleeping. At St Omer our craving for an omelette nearly lost us the bus. Then we slept. All that I can remember of the rest of the journey is that we stopped near Bailleul. An anxious corporal popped his head in.

"Mr Brown here?"

"Ye—e—s," sleepily, "what the devil do you want?"

"Our battery's in action, sir, a few miles from here. I've got your horses ready waiting, sir."

Mr Brown was thoroughly awake in a moment. He disturbed everybody collecting his kit. Then he vanished.

We were late at Bailleul, and there was no one to meet us. The Cyclists as usual came to our help. Their gig was waiting, and climbing into it we drove furiously to St Jans Cappel. Making some sort of beds for ourselves, we fell asleep. When we woke up in the morning our leave was a dream.

Chapter 11
St Jans Cappel

Soon after our return there were rumours of a grand attack. Headquarters positively sizzled with the most expensive preparations. At a given word the Staff were to dash out in motor-cars to a disreputable tavern, so that they could see the shells bursting. A couple of despatch riders were to keep with them in order to fetch their cars when the day's work was over. A mobile reserve of motor-cyclists was to be established in a farm under cover.

The whole scheme was perfect. There was good rabbit-shooting near the tavern. The atmosphere inside was so thick that it actually induced slumber. The landlady possessed an excellent stove, upon which the Staff's lunch, prepared with quiet genius at St Jans, might be heated up. The place was dirty enough to give all those in authority, who might come round to see that the British Army was really doing something, a vivid conception of the horrors of war. And, as I have said, there was a slope behind the road from which lots and lots of shells could be seen bursting.

The word came. We arrived at the tavern before dawn. The Staff sauntered about outside in delicious anticipation. We all looked at our watches. Punctually at six the show began. Guns of all shapes and sizes had been concentrated. They made an overwhelming noise. Over the German trenches on the near slope of the Messines ridge flashed multitudinous points of flame. The Germans were being furiously shelled. The dawn came up while the Staff were drinking their matutinal tea. The Staff set itself sternly to work. Messages describing events at La Bassée poured in. They were conscientiously read and rushed over the wires to our brigades. The guns were making more noise than they had ever made before. The Germans were cowering in their trenches. It was all our officers could do to hold back their men, who were straining like hounds in a leash to get at the hated foe. A shell fell among some of the gunners' transport and wounded a man and two horses. That stiffened us. The news was flashed over the wire to G.H.Q. The transport was moved rapidly, but in good order, to a safer place. The guns fired more furiously than ever.

As soon as there was sufficient light, the General's A.D.C., crammed full of the lust for blood, went out and shot some rabbits and some indescribable birds, who by this time were petrified with fear. They had never heard such a noise before. That other despatch rider sat comfortably in a car, finished at his leisure the second volume of 'Sinister Street,' and wrote a lurid description of a modern battle.

Before the visitors came, the scene was improved by the construction of a large dug-out near the tavern. It is true that if the Staff had taken to the dug-out they would most certainly have been drowned. That did not matter. Every well-behaved Divisional Staff must have a dug-out near its Advanced Headquarters. It is always "done."

Never was a Division so lucky in its visitors. A certain young prince of high lineage arrived. Everybody saluted at the same time. He was, I think, duly impressed by the atmosphere of the tavern, the sight of the Staff's maps, the inundated dug-outs, the noise of the guns and the funny balls of smoke that the shells made when they exploded over the German lines.

What gave this battle a humorous twist for all time was the delectable visit of a Cabinet Minister. He came in a car and brought with him his own knife and fork and a loaf of bread as his contribution to the Divisional Lunch. When he entered the tavern he smelt among other smells the delicious odour of rabbit-pie. With hurried but charming condescension he left his loaf on the stove, where it dried for a day or two until the landlady had the temerity to appropriate it. He was fed, so far as I remember on—soup, fish, rabbit-pie, potatoes, cabbage, apple-tart, fruit, coffee, liqueurs; and after lunch, I am told, showed a marked disinclination to ascend the hill and watch the shells bursting. He was only a "civvy."[25]

The battle lasted about ten days. Each morning the Staff, like lazy men who are "something in the city," arrived a little later at the tavern. Each afternoon they departed a little earlier. The rabbits decreased in number, and finally, when two days running the A.D.C. had been able to shoot nothing at all, the Division returned for good to the Chateau at St Jans Cappel.

For this mercy the despatch riders were truly grateful. Sitting the whole day in the tavern, we had all contracted bad headaches. Even chess, the *Red Magazine*, and the writing of letters, could do nothing to dissipate our unutterable boredom. Never did we pass that tavern afterwards without a shudder of disgust. With joyous content we heard a month or two later that it had been closed for providing drinks after hours.

Officially the grand attack had taken this course. The French to the north had been held up by the unexpected strength of the German defence. The 3rd Division on our immediate left had advanced a trifle, for the Gordons had made a perilous charge into the Petit Bois, a wood at the bottom of the Wytschaete Heights. And the Royal Scots had put in some magnificent work, for which they were afterwards very properly congratulated. The Germans in front of our Division were so cowed by our magniloquent display of gunnery that they have remained moderately quiet ever since.

After these December manoeuvres nothing of importance happened on our front until the spring, when the Germans, whom we had tickled with intermittent gunnery right through the winter, began to retaliate with a certain energy.

The Division that has no history is not necessarily happy. There were portions of the line, it is true, which provided a great deal of comfort and very little danger. Fine dug-outs were constructed—you have probably seen them in the illustrated papers. The men were more at home in such trenches than in the ramshackle farms behind the lines. These show trenches were emphatically the exception. The average trench on the line dur-

25. The soldier's contemptuous expression for the inhabitants of the civilian world.

ing last winter was neither comfortable nor safe. Yellow clay, six inches to four feet or more of stinking water, many corpses behind the trenches buried just underneath the surface-crust, and in front of the trenches not buried at all, inveterate sniping from a slightly superior position—these are not pleasant bedfellows. The old Division (or rather the new Division—the infantrymen of the old Division were now pitifully few) worked right hard through the winter. When the early spring came and the trenches were dry, the Division was sent north to bear a hand in the two bloodiest actions of the war. So far as I know, in the whole history of British participation in this war there has never been a more murderous fight than one of these two actions—and the Division, with slight outside help, managed the whole affair.

Twice in the winter there was an attempted *rapprochement* between the Germans and ourselves. The more famous gave the Division a mention by "Eyewitness," so we all became swollen with pride.

On the Kaiser's birthday one-and-twenty large shells were dropped accurately into a farm suspected of being a battalion or brigade headquarters. The farm promptly acknowledged the compliment by blowing up, and all round it little explosions followed. Nothing pleases a gunner more than to strike a magazine. He always swears he knew it was there the whole time, and, as gunners are dangerous people to quarrel with, we always pretended to believe the tale.

There are many people in England still who cannot stomach the story of the Christmas truce. "Out there," we cannot understand why. Good fighting men respect good fighting men. On our front, and on the fronts of other divisions, the Germans had behaved throughout the winter with a passable gentlemanliness. Besides, neither the British nor the German soldier—with the possible exception of the Prussians—has been able to stoke up that virulent hate which devastates so many German and British homes. A certain lance-corporal puts the matter thus:[26]—

26. I retired with some haste from Flanders the night after the Germans first began to use gas. Militant chemistry may have altered the British soldier's convictions.

"We're fightin' for somethink what we've got. Those poor beggars is fightin' cos they've got to. An' old Bill Kayser's fightin' for somethin' what 'e'll never get. But 'e will get somethink, and that's a good 'iding!"[27]

We even had a sneaking regard for that "cunning old bird, Kayser Bill." Our treatment of prisoners explains the Christmas Truce. The British soldier, except when he is smarting under some dirty trick, suffering under terrible loss, or maddened by fighting or fatigue, treats his prisoners with a tolerant, rather contemptuous kindness. May God in His mercy help any poor German who falls into the hands of a British soldier when the said German has "done the dirty" or has "turned nasty"! There is no judge so remorseless, no executioner so ingenious in making the punishment fit the crime.

This is what I wrote home a day or two after Christmas: From six on Christmas Eve to six in the evening on Christmas Day there was a truce between two regiments of our Division and the Germans opposite them. Heads popped up and were not sniped. Greetings were called across. One venturesome, enthusiastic German got out of his trench and stood waving a branch of Christmas Tree. Soon there was a fine pow-wow going on. Cigars were exchanged for tobacco. Friendship was pledged in socks. The Germans brought out some beer and the English some rum. Finally, on Christmas Day, there was a great concert and dance. The Germans were spruce, elderly men, keen and well fed, with buttons cleaned for the occasion. They appeared to have plenty of supplies, and were fully equipped with everything necessary for a winter campaign. A third battalion, wisely but churlishly, refused these seasonable advances, and shot four men who appeared with a large cask of what was later discovered to be beer....

"The Div." were billeted in a chateau on the slope of a hill three-quarters of a mile above St Jans Cappel. This desirable residence stands in two acres of garden, just off the road. At the gate was a lodge. Throughout the winter we despatch riders lived in two small rooms of this lodge. We averaged fourteen in number.

27. I have left out the usual monotonous epithet. Any soldier can supply it.

Two were out with the brigades, leaving twelve to live, eat, and sleep in two rooms, each about 15 ft. by 8 ft. We were distinctly cramped, and cursed the day that had brought us to St Jans. It was a cruel stroke that gave us for our winter quarters the worst billets we had ever suffered.

As we became inclined to breakfast late, nine o'clock parade was instituted. Breakfast took place before or after, as the spirit listed. Bacon, tea, and bread came from the cook. We added porridge and occasionally eggs. The porridge we half-cooked the night before.

After breakfast we began to clean our bicycles, no light task, and the artificers started on repairs. The cleaning process was usually broken into by the arrival of the post and the papers of the day before. Cleaning the bicycles, sweeping out the rooms, reading and writing letters, brought us to dinner at 1.

This consisted of bully or fresh meat stew with vegetables (or occasionally roast or fried meat), bread and jam. As we became more luxurious we would provide for ourselves Yorkshire pudding, which we discovered trying to make pancakes, and pancakes, which we discovered trying to make Yorkshire pudding. Worcester Sauce and the invaluable curry powder were never wanting. After dinner we smoked a lethargic pipe.

In the afternoon it was customary to take some exercise. To reduce the strain on our back tyres we used to trudge manfully down into the village, or, if we were feeling energetic, to the ammunition column a couple of miles away. Any distance over two miles we covered on motor-cycles. Their use demoralised us. Our legs shrunk away.

Sometimes two or three of us would ride to a sand-pit on Mont Noir and blaze away with our revolvers. Incidentally, not one of us had fired a shot in anger since the war began. We treated our revolvers as unnecessary luggage. In time we became skilled in their use, and thereafter learnt to keep them moderately clean. We had been served out with revolvers at Chatham, but had never practised with them—except at Carlow for a morning, and then we were suffering from the effects of inoculation. They may be useful when we get to Germany.

Shopping in Bailleul was less strenuous. We were always buying something for supper—a kilo of liver, some onions, a few sausages—anything that could be cooked by the unskilled on a paraffin-stove. Then after shopping there were cafés we could drop into, sure of a welcome. It was impossible to live from November to March "within easy reach of town" and not make friends.

Milk for tea came from the farm in which No. 1 Section of the Signal Company was billeted. When first we were quartered at St Jans this section wallowed in some mud a little above the chateau.

Because I had managed to make myself understood to some German prisoners, I was looked upon as a great linguist, and vulgarly credited with a knowledge of all the European languages. So I was sent, together with the Quartermaster-Sergeant and the Sergeant-Major, on billeting expeditions. Arranging for quarters at the farm, I made great friends with the farmer. He was a tall, thin, lithe old man, with a crumpled wife and prodigiously large family. He was a man of affairs, too, for once a month in peace time he would drive into Hazebrouck. While his wife got me the milk, we used to sit by the fire and smoke our pipes and discuss the terrible war and the newspapers. One of the most embarrassing moments I have ever experienced was when he bade me tell the sergeants that he regarded them as brothers, and loved them all. I said it first in French, that he might hear, and then in English. The sergeants blushed, while the old man beamed.

We loved the Flemish, and, for the most part, they loved us. When British soldiers arrived in a village the men became clean, the women smart, and the boys inevitably procured putties and wore them with pride. The British soldier is certainly not insular. He tries hard to understand the words and ways of his neighbours. He has a rough tact, a crude courtesy, and a great-hearted generosity. In theory no task could be more difficult than the administration of the British Area. Even a friendly military occupation is an uncomfortable burden. Yet never have I known any case of real ill-feeling. Personally, during my nine months at the Front, I have always received from the French and the Belgians amazing kindness and consideration. As an officer I came into contact with village and town officials over questions of billets and requisitions. In any difficulty I received courteous assistance. No trouble was too great; no time was too valuable....

After tea of cakes and rolls the bridge-players settled down to a quiet game, with pipes to hand and whisky and siphons on the sideboard. We took it in turns to cook some delicacy for supper at 8—sausages, curried sardines, liver and bacon, or—rarely but joyously—fish. At one time or another we feasted on all the luxuries, but fish was rarer than rubies. When we had it we did not care if we stank out the whole lodge with odours of its frying. We would lie down to sleep content in a thick fishy, paraffin-y, dripping-y atmosphere. When I came home I could not think what the delicious smell was in a certain street. Then my imagination struck out a picture—Grimers laboriously frying a dab over a smoky paraffin-stove.

On occasions after supper we would brew a large jorum of good rum-punch, sing songs with roaring choruses, and finish up the evening with a good old scrap over somebody else's bed. The word went round to "mobilise," and we would all stand ready, each on his bed, to repel boarders. If the sanctity of your bed were violated, the intruder would be cast vigorously into outer darkness. Another song, another drink, a final pipe, and to bed.

Our Christmas would have been a grand day if it had not been away from home.

At eight o'clock there was breakfast of porridge, bacon and eggs, and bloaters—everybody in the best of spirits. About nine the Skipper presented us with cards from the King and Queen. Then the mail came in, but it was poor. By the time we had tidied up our places and done a special Christmas shave and wash, we were called upon to go down to the cookhouse and sign for Princess Mary's Christmas gift—a good pipe, and in a pleasant little brass box lay a Christmas card, a photograph, a packet of cigarettes, and another of excellent tobacco.

It was now lunch-time—steak and potatoes.

The afternoon was spent on preparations for our great and unexampled dinner. Grimers printed the menu, and while I made some cold curried sardines, the rest went down into the village to stimulate the landlady of the inn where we were going to dine.

In the village a brigade was billeted, and that brigade was, of course, "on the wire." It was arranged that the despatch riders next on the list should take their motor-cycles down and be summoned over the wire if they were needed. An order had come round that unimportant messages were to be kept until the morning.

We dined in the large kitchen of the *Maison Commune Estaminet*, at a long table decorated with mistletoe and holly. The dinner—the result of two days' "scrounging" under the direction of George—was too good to be true. We toasted each other and sang all the songs we knew. Two of the Staff clerks wandered in and told us we were the best of all possible despatch riders. We drank to them uproariously. Then a Scotsman turned up with a noisy recitation. Finally, we all strolled home up the hill singing loudly and pleasantly, very exhilarated, in sure and certain belief we had spent the best of all possible evenings.

In the dwelling of the Staff there was noise of revelry. Respectable captains with false noses peered out of windows. Our Fat Boy declaimed in the signal office on the iniquities of the artillery telegraphists. Sadders sent gentle messages of greeting over the wires. He was still a little piqued at his failure to secure the piper of the K.O.S.B., who had been commandeered by the Staff. Sadders waited for him until early morning and then steered him to our lodge, but the piper was by then too tired to play.

Here is our bill of fare—

Christmas, 1914 dinner of the
Ten Surviving Motor-Cyclists of
the Famous Fifth Division

Sardins très Moutard
Potage
Dindon Rôti-Saucisses. Oise Rôti
Petits Choux de Bruxelles
Pommes de Terre

Pouding de Noël Rhum
Dessert
Café
Liqueurs
Vins: Champagne, Moselle, Port
Benedictine
Whisky

On the reverse page we put our battle-honours—Mons, Le Cateau, Crêpy-en-Valois, the Marne, the Aisne, La Bassée, the Defence of Ypres.[28]

We beat the Staff on the sprouts, but the Staff countered by appropriating the piper.

Work dwindled until it became a farce. One run for each despatch rider every third day was the average. St Jans was not the place we should have chosen for a winter resort. Life became monotonous, and we all with one accord began applying for commissions. Various means were used to break the monotony. Grimers, under the Skipper's instructions, began to plant vegetables for the spring, but I do not think he ever got much beyond mustard and cress. On particularly unpleasant days we were told off to make fascines. N'Soon assisted the Quartermaster-Sergeant. Cecil did vague things with the motor-lorry. I was called upon to write the Company's War Diary. Even the Staff became restless and took to night-walks behind the trenches. If it had not been for the generous supply of "days off" that the Skipper allowed us, we should by February have begun to gibber.

Despatches were of two kinds—ordinary and priority. "Priority" despatches could only be sent by the more important members of the Staff. They were supposed to be important, were marked "priority" in the corner, and taken at once in a hurry. Ordinary despatches went by the morning and evening posts. During the winter a regular system of motor-cyclist posts was organised right through the British Area. A message could be sent from Neuve Eglise to Chartres in about two days. Our

28. To these may now be added—St Eloi, Hill 60, the Second Battle of Ypres.

posts formed the first or last stage of the journey. The morning post left at 7.30 a.m., and the evening at 3.30 p.m. All the units of the division were visited.

If the roads were moderately good and no great movements of troops were proceeding, the post took about 1-1/4 hours; so the miserable postman was late either for breakfast or for tea. It was routine work pure and simple. After six weeks we knew every stone in the roads. The postman never came under fire. He passed through one village which was occasionally shelled, but, while I was with the Signal Company, the postman and the shells never arrived at the village at the same time. There was far more danger from lorries and motor ambulances than from shells.

As for the long line of "postmen" that stretched back into the dim interior of France—it was rarely that they even heard the guns. When they did hear them, they would, I am afraid, pluck a racing helmet from their pockets, draw the ear-flaps well down over their ears, bend down over their racing handle-bars, and sprint for dear life. Returning safely to Abbéville, they would write hair-raising accounts of the dangers they had passed through to the motor-cycling papers. It is only right that I should here once and for all confess—there is no finer teller of tall stories than the motor-cyclist despatch rider....

From December to February the only time I was under shell fire was late in December, when the Grand Attack was in full train. A certain brigade headquarters had taken refuge inconsiderately in advanced dug-outs. As I passed along the road to them some shrapnel was bursting a quarter of a mile away. So long was it since I had been under fire that the noise of our own guns disturbed me. In the spring, after I had left the Signal Company, the roads were not so healthy. George experienced the delights of a broken chain on a road upon which the Germans were registering accurately with shrapnel. Church, a fine fellow, and quite the most promising of our recruits, was killed in his billet by a shell when attached to a brigade.

Taking the post rarely meant just a pleasant spin, because it rained in Flanders from September to January.

One day I started out from D.H.Q. at 3.30 p.m. with the afternoon post, and reached the First Brigade well up to time. Then it began to rain, at first slightly, and then very heavily indeed, with a bagful of wind. On a particularly open stretch of road—the rain was stinging sharply—the engine stopped. With a heroic effort I tugged the bicycle through some mud to the side of a shed, in the hope that when the wind changed—it did not—I might be under cover. I could not see. I could not grip—and of course I could not find out what the matter was.

After I had been working for about half an hour the two artillery motor-cyclists came along. I stopped them to give me a hand and to do as much work as I could possibly avoid doing myself while preserving an appearance of omniscience.

We worked for an hour or more. It was now so dark that I could not distinguish one motor-cyclist from another. The rain rained faster than it had ever rained before, and the gale was so violent that we could scarcely keep our feet. Finally, we diagnosed a complaint that could not be cured by the roadside. So we stopped working, to curse and admire the German rockets.

There was an estaminet close by. It had appeared shut, but when we began to curse a light shone in one of the windows. So I went in and settled to take one of the artillery motor-cycles and deliver the rest of my quite unimportant despatches. It would not start. We worked for twenty minutes in the rain vainly, then a motor-cyclist turned up from the nearest brigade to see what had become of me—the progress of the post is checked over the wire. We arranged matters—but then neither his motor-cycle nor the motor-cycle of the second artillery motor-cyclist would start. It was laughable. Eventually we got the brigade despatch rider started with my report.

A fifth motor-cyclist, who discreetly did not stop his engine, took my despatches back to "the Div." The second artillery motor-cycle we started after quarter of an hour's prodigious labour. The first and mine were still obstinate, so he and I retired to the inn, drank brandy and hot water, and conversed amiably with *madame*.

Madame, who together with innumerable old men and children inhabited the inn, was young and pretty and intelligent—black hair, sallow and symmetrical face, expressive mouth, slim and graceful limbs. Talking the language, we endeavoured to make our forced company pleasant. That other despatch rider, still steaming from the stove, sat beside a charming Flemish woman, and endeavoured, amid shrieks of laughter, to translate the jokes in an old number of *London Opinion*.

A Welsh lad came in—a perfect Celt of nineteen, dark and lithe, with a momentary smile and a wild desire to see India. Then some Cheshires arrived. They were soaked and very weary. One old reservist staggered to a chair. We gave him some brandy and hot water. He chattered unintelligibly for a moment about his wife and children. He began to doze, so his companion took him out, and they tottered along after their company.

A dog of no possible breed belonged to the estaminet. *Madame* called him Automobile Anglais, because he was always rushing about for no conceivable reason.

We were sorry when at 9.50 the lorry came for the bicycles. Our second driver was an ex-London cabby, with a crude wit expressed in impossible French that our hostess delightfully parried. On the way back he told me how he had given up the three taxis he had owned to do "his bit," how the other men had laughed at him because he was so old, how he had met a prisoner who used to whistle for the taxis in Russell Square. We talked also of the men in the trenches, of fright, and of the end of the war. We reached D.H.Q. about 10.30, and after a large bowl of porridge I turned in.

CHAPTER 12

Behind the Lines

I had intended to write down a full description of the country immediately behind our present line. The Skipper, for fear we should become stale, allowed us plenty of leave. We would make little expeditions to Béthune for the baths, spend an afternoon riding round Armentières, or run over to Poperinghe for a chop. We even arranged for a visit to the Belgian lines, but that excursion was forbidden by a new order. Right through the winter we had "unrivalled opportunities"—as the journalists would say—of becoming intimate with that strip of Flanders which extends from Ypres to Béthune. Whether I can or may describe it is a matter for care. A too affectionate description of the neighbourhood of Wulverghem, for instance, would be unwise. But I see no reason why I should not state as a fact that a most excellent dry Martini could be obtained in Ypres up to the evening of April 22.

Wretched Ypres has been badly over-written. Before the war it was a pleasant city, little visited by travellers because it lay on a badly served branch line. The inhabitants tell me it was never much troubled with tourists. One burgher explained the situation to me with a comical mixture of sentiment and reason.

"You see, sir, that our Cathedral is shattered and the Cloth Hall a ruin. May those devils, the dirty Germans, roast in Hell! But after the war we shall be the richest city in Belgium. All England will flock to Ypres. Is it not a monstrous cemetery? Are there not woods and villages and farms at which the brave English have fought like lions to earn for themselves eternal fame, and for the city an added glory? The good God gives His compensations after great wars. There will be many to buy our lace and fill our restaurants."

Mr John Buchan and Mr Valentine Williams and others have "written up" Ypres. The exact state of the Cloth Hall at any given moment is the object of solicitude. The shattered Belgian homes have been described over and over again. The important things about Ypres have been left unsaid.

Near the station there was a man who really could mix cocktails. He was no blundering amateur, but an expert with the subtlest touch. And in the Rue de Lille a fashionable dressmaker turned her *atelier* into a tea-room. She used to provide coffee or chocolate, or even tea, and the most delicious little cakes. Of an afternoon you would sit on comfortable chairs at a neat table covered with a fair cloth and talk to your hostess. A few hats daintily remained on stands, but, as she said, they were last year's hats, unworthy of our notice.

A pleasant afternoon could be spent on the old ramparts. We were there, as a matter of fact, to do a little building-up and clearing-away when the German itch for destruction proved too strong for their more gentlemanly feelings. We lay on the grass in the sun and smoked our pipes, looking across the placid moat to Zillebeke Vyver, Verbranden Molen, and the slight curve of Hill 60. The landscape was full of interest. Here was shrapnel bursting over entirely empty fields. There was a sapper repairing a line. The Germans were shelling the town, and it was a matter of skill to decide when the lumbersome old shell was heard exactly where it would fall. Then we would walk back into the town for tea and look in at that particularly enterprising grocer's in the Square to see his latest novelties in tinned goods.

From Ypres the best road in Flanders runs by Vlamertinghe to Poperinghe. It is a good macadam road, made, doubtless by perfidious Albion's money, just before the war.

Poperinghe has been an age-long rival of Ypres. Even to-day its inhabitants delight to tell you the old municipal scandals of the larger town, and the burghers of Ypres, if they see a citizen of Poperinghe in their streets, believe he has come to gloat over their misfortunes. Ypres is an Edinburgh and Poperinghe a Glasgow. Ypres was self-consciously "old world" and loved its buildings. Poperinghe is modern, and perpetrated a few years ago the most terrible of town halls. There are no cocktails in Poperinghe, but there is good whisky and most excellent beer.

I shall never forget my feelings when one morning in a certain wine-merchant's cellar I saw several eighteen-gallon casks of Bass's Pale Ale. I left Poperinghe in a motor-ambulance, and the Germans shelled it next day, but my latest advices state that the ale is still intact.

Across the road from the wine-merchant's is a delectable tea-shop. There is a tea-shop at Bailleul, the Allies Tea-Rooms. It was started early in March. It is full of bad blue china and inordinately expensive. Of the tea-shop at Poperinghe I cannot speak too highly. There is a vast variety of the most delicious cakes. The proprietress is pleasant and her maids are obliging. It is also cheap. I have only one fault to find with it—the room is small. Infantry officers walk miles into Poperinghe for their tea and then find the room crowded with those young subalterns who supply us with our bully. They bring in bulldogs and stay a long time.

Dickebusch used to be a favourite Sunday afternoon's ride for the Poperinghe wheelers. They would have tea at the restaurant on the north of Dickebusch Vyver, and afterwards go for a row in the little flat-bottomed boats, accompanied, no doubt, by some nice dark Flemish girls. The village, never very pleasant, is now the worse for wear. I remember it with no kindly feelings, because, having spent a night there with the French, I left them in the morning too early to obtain a satisfactory meal, and arrived at Headquarters too late for any breakfast.

Not far from Dickebusch is the Desolate Chateau. Before the war it was a handsome place, built by a rich coal-merchant from Lille. I visited it on a sunny morning. At the southern gate there was a little black and shapeless heap fluttering a rag in the wind. I saluted and passed on, sick at heart. The grounds were pitted with shell-holes: the cucumber-frames were shattered. Just behind the chateau was a wee village of dug-outs. Now they are slowly falling in. And the chateau itself?

It had been so proud of its finery, its pseudo-Greek columns, and its rich furnishings. Battered and confused—there is not a room of it which is not open to the wind from the sea. The pictures lie prostrate on the floor before their ravisher. The curtains are torn and faded. The papers of its master are scattered over the carpet and on the rifled desk. In the bedroom of its mistress her linen has been thrown about wildly; yet her two silver brushes still lie on the dressing-table. Even the children's room had been pillaged, and the books, torn and defaced, lay in a rough heap.

All was still. At the foot of the garden there was a little village half hidden by trees. Not a sound came from it. Away on the ridge miserable Wytschaete stood hard against the sky, a mass of trembling ruins. Then two soldiers came, and finding a boat rowed noisily round the tiny lake, and the shells murmured harshly as they flew across to Ypres. Some ruins are dead stones, but the broken houses of Flanders are pitifully alive—like the wounded men who lie between the trenches and cannot be saved....

Half a mile south from Dickebusch are cross-roads, and the sign-post tells you that the road to the left is the road to Wytschaete—but Wytschaete faces Kemmel and Messines faces Wulverghem.

I was once walking over the hills above Witzenhausen—the cherries by the roadside were wonderful that year—and coming into a valley we asked a man how we might best strike a path into the next valley over the shoulder of the hill. He said he did not know, because he had never been over the hill. The people of the next valley were strangers to him. When first I came to a sign-post that told me how to get to a village I could not reach with my life, I thought of those hills above Witzenhausen. From Wulverghem to Messines is exactly two kilometres. It is ludicrous.

Again, one afternoon I was riding over the pass between Mont Noir and Mont Vidaigne. I looked to the east and saw in the distance the smoke of a train, just as from Harrow you might see the Scottish Express on the North-Western main line. For a moment I did not realise that the train was German, that the purpose of its journey was to kill me and my fellow-men. But it is too easy to sentimentalise, to labour the stark fact that war is a grotesque, irrational absurdity....

Following the main road south from Dickebusch you cross the frontier and come to Bailleul, a town of which we were heartily sick before the winter was far gone. In peace it would be once seen and never remembered. It has no character, though I suppose the Faucon is as well known to Englishmen now as any hotel in Europe. There are better shops in Béthune and better cafés in Poperinghe. Of the Allies Tea-Rooms I have already written.

Bailleul is famous for one thing alone—its baths. Just outside the town is a large and modern asylum that contains a good plunge-bath for the men and gorgeous hot baths for officers. There are none better behind the line. Tuesdays and Fridays were days of undiluted joy.

Armentières is sprawling and ugly and full of dirt—a correct and middle-class town that reminded me of Bristol. In front of it are those trenches, of which many tales wandered up and down the line. Here the Christmas truce is said to have been prolonged for three weeks or more. Here the men are supposed to prefer their comfortable trenches to their billets, though when they "come out" they are cheered by the Follies and the Fancies. On this section of the line is the notorious Plugstreet Wood, that show-place to which all distinguished but valuable visitors are taken. Other corps have sighed for the gentle delights of this section of the line....

South-west from Armentières the country is as level as it can be. It is indeed possible to ride from Ypres to Béthune without meeting any hill except the slight ascent from La Clytte. Steenwerck, Erquinghem, Croix du Bac, and, farther west, Merris and Vieux Berquin, have no virtue whatsoever. There is little country flatter and uglier than the country between Bailleul and Béthune.

One morning Huggie, Cecil, and I obtained leave to visit Béthune and the La Bassée district. It was in the middle of January, three months after we had left Beuvry. We tore into Bailleul and bumped along the first mile of the Armentières road. That mile is without any doubt the most excruciatingly painful *pavé* in the world. We crossed the railway and raced south. The roads were good and there was little traffic, but the sudden apparition of a motor-lorry round a sharp corner sent that other despatch rider into the ditch. Estaires, as always, produced much grease. It began to rain, but we held on by La Gorgue and Lestrem, halting only once for the necessary café-cognac.

We were stopped for our passes at the bridge into Béthune by a private of the London Scottish. I rejoiced exceedingly, and finding Alec, took him off to a bath and then to the restaurant where I had breakfasted when first we came to Béthune. The meal was as good as it had been three months before, and the flapper as charming.[29] After lunch we had our hair cut. Then Cecil took us to the little blue-and-white café for tea. She did play the piano, but two subalterns of the less combatant type came in and put us to flight. A corporal is sometimes at such a disadvantage.

We rode along the canal bank to Beuvry Station, and found that our filthy old quarters had been cleaned up and turned into an Indian dressing-station. We went on past the cross-roads at Gorre, where an Indian battalion was waiting miserably under the dripping trees. The sun was just setting behind some grey clouds. The fields were flooded with ochreous water. Since last I had been along the road the country had been "searched" too thoroughly. One wall of 1910 farm remained. Chickens pecked feebly among the rest of it.

Coming into Festubert I felt that something was wrong. The village had been damnably shelled—that I had expected—and there was not a soul to be seen. I thought of the father and mother and daughter who, returning to their home while we were there in October, had wept because a fuse had gone through the door and the fireplace and all their glass had been broken. Their house was now a heap of nothing in particular. The mirror I had used lay broken on the top of about quarter of a wall. Still something was wrong, and Huggie, who had been smiling at my puzzled face, said gently in an off-hand way—

29. I cannot remember the name of the restaurant. Go to the north-east corner of the Square and turn down a lane to your right. It is the fourth or fifth house on your right. In Béthune there is also, of course, the big hotel where generals lunch. If you find the company of generals a little trying go to the flapper's restaurant.

"Seen the church?"

That was it! The church had simply disappeared. In the old days riding up from Gorre the fine tower of the church rose above the houses at the end of the street. The tower had been shelled and had fallen crashing through the roof.

We met a sapper coming out of a cottage. He was rather amused at our sentimental journey, and warned us that the trenches were considerably nearer the village than they had been in our time. We determined to push on as it was now dusk, but my engine jibbed, and we worked on it in the gloom among the dark and broken houses. The men in the trenches roused themselves to a sleepless night, and intermittent rifle-shots rang out in the damp air.

We rode north to the Estaminet de l'Epinette, passing a road which forking to the right led to a German barricade. The estaminet still lived, but farther down the road the old house which had sheltered a field ambulance was a pile of rubbish. On we rode by La Couture to Estaires, where we dined, and so to St Jans Cappel....

Do you know what the Line means? When first we came to Landrecies the thought of the Frontier as something strong and stark had thrilled us again and again, but the Frontier was feeble and is nothing. A man of Poperinghe told me his brother was professor, his son was serving, his wife and children were "over there." He pointed to the German lines. Of his wife and children he has heard nothing for four months. Some of us are fighting to free "German" Flanders, the country where life is dark and bitter. Those behind our line, however confident they may be, live in fear, for if the line were to retire a little some of them would be cast into the bitter country. A day will come "when the whole line will advance," and the welcome we shall receive then from those who have come out of servitude!... There are men and women in France who live only for that day, just as there are those in this country who would welcome the day of death, so that they might see again those they love....

You may have gathered from my former letters that no friction took place between the professional and amateur soldiers of the Signal Company. I have tried all through my letters to give you a very truthful idea of our life, and my account would not be complete without some description of the Signal Company and its domestic affairs.

Think for a moment of what happened at the beginning of August. More than a dozen 'Varsity men were thrown like Daniels into a den of mercenaries. We were awkwardly privileged persons—full corporals with a few days' service. Motor-cycling gave superlative opportunities of freedom. Our duties were "flashy," and brought us into familiar contact with officers of rank. We were highly paid, and thought to have much money of our own. In short, we who were soldiers of no standing possessed the privileges that a professional soldier could win only after many years' hard work.

Again, it did not help matters that our Corps was a Corps of intelligent experts who looked down on the ordinary "Tommy," that our Company had deservedly the reputation of being one of the best Signal Companies in the Army—a reputation which has been enhanced and duly rewarded in the present war. These motor-cyclists were not only experimental interlopers. They might even "let down" the Company.

We expected jealousy and unpleasantness, which we hoped to overcome by hard work. We found a tactful kindness that was always smoothing the rough way, helping us amusedly, and giving us more than our due, and a thorough respect where respect was deserved. It was astonishing, but then we did not know the professional soldier. During the winter there was a trifle of friction over cooking, the work of the Signal Office, and the use and abuse of motor-cycles. It would have been a poor-spirited company if there had been none. But the friction was transitory, and left no acid feeling.

I should like to pay my compliments to a certain commanding officer, but six months' work under him has convinced me that he does not like compliments. Still, there remains that dinner at the end of the war, and then...!

The Sergeant-Major frightened us badly at first. He looked so much like a Sergeant-Major, and a Sergeant-Major is more to be feared than the C.O., or the General, or the A.P.M., or anybody else in this disciplinary world. He can make life Hell or Heaven or a judicious compromise. Our Sergeant-Major believed in the judicious compromise with a tendency towards Heaven. When any question arose between professional and amateur, he dealt with it impartially. At other times he was inclined to let us work out our own salvation. I have always had a mighty respect for the Sergeant-Major, but have never dared tell him so. Perhaps he will read this.

The "Quarter-Bloke"[30] was a jewel. He was suddenly called upon to keep us supplied with things of which he had never even heard the names. He rose to the occasion like a hero or Mr Selfridge's buyer. Never did he pass by an unconsidered trifle. One day a rumour went round that we might get side-cars. That was enough for the Quarter-Bloke. He picked up every large-sized tyre he thought might come in useful. The side-cars came. There was a rush for tyres. The Quarter-Bloke did not rush. He only smiled.

His great triumph was the affair of the leather jackets. A maternal Government thought to send us out leather jackets. After tea the Q.-B. bustled in with them. We rode out with them the next morning. The 2nd Corps had not yet received theirs. We were the first motor-cyclists in our part of the world to appear in flaring chrome. The Q.-B. smiled again.

I always think the Quarter-Bloke is wasted. He ought to be put in charge of the Looting Department of a large invading army. Do not misunderstand me. The Q.-B. never "looted." He never stepped a hair's-breadth outside those regulations that hedge round the Quartermaster. He was just a man with a prophetic instinct, who, while others passed blindly by, picked up things because they might come in useful some day—and they always did. Finally, the Q.-B. was companionable. He could tell a good story, and make merry decorously, as befitted a Company Quartermaster-Sergeant.

Of the other sergeants I will make no individual mention. We took some for better, and some for worse, but they were all good men, who knew their job.

---

30. Company Quartermaster-Sergeant, now a Sergeant-Major.

Then there was "Ginger," the cook. I dare not describe his personal appearance lest I should meet him again—and I want to—but it was remarkable. So was his language. One of us had a fair gift that way, and duels were frequent, but "Ginger" always had the last word. He would keep in reserve a monstrously crude sulphurous phrase with a sting of humour in its tail, and, when our fellow had concluded triumphantly with an exotic reference to Ginger's hereditary characteristics, Ginger would hesitate a moment, as if thinking, and then out with *it*. Obviously there was no more to be said.

I have ever so much more to tell about the Signal Company in detail and dialogue. Perhaps some day I shall have the courage to say it, but I shall be careful to hide about whom I am writing....

The "commission fever," which we had caught on the Aisne and, more strongly, at Beuvry, swept over us late in January. Moulders, who had lost his own company and joined on to us during the Retreat, had retired into the quietude of the A.S.C. Cecil was selected to go home and train the despatch riders of the New Armies.

There were points in being "an officer and a gentleman." Dirt and discomfort were all very well when there was plenty of work to do, and we all decided that every officer should have been in the ranks, but despatch-riding had lost its savour. We had become postmen. Thoughts of the days when we had dashed round picking-up brigades, had put battalions on the right road, and generally made ourselves conspicuous, if not useful, discontented us. So we talked it over.

Directing the operations of a very large gun seemed a good job. There would not be much moving to do, because monster guns were notoriously immobile. Hours are regular; the food is good, and can generally be eaten in comparative safety. If the gun had a very long range it would be quite difficult to hit. Unfortunately gunnery is a very technical job, and requires some acquaintance with Algebra. So we gave up the idea.

We did not dote on the cavalry, for many reasons. First, when cavalry is not in action it does nothing but clean its stables and exercise its horses. Second, if ever we broke through the German lines the cavalry would probably go ahead of anybody else. Third, we could not ride very well, and the thought of falling off in front of our men when they were charging daunted us.

The sappers required brains, and we had too great an admiration for the infantry to attempt commanding them. Besides, they walked and lived in trenches.

Two of us struck upon a corps which combined the advantages of every branch of the service. We drew up a list of each other's qualifications to throw a sop to modesty, sent in our applications, and waited. At the same time we adopted a slight tone of hauteur towards those who were not potential officers.

One night after tea "Ginger" brought in the orders. I had become a gentleman, and, saying good-bye, I walked down into the village and reported myself to the officer commanding the Divisional Cyclists. I was no longer a despatch rider but a very junior subaltern.

I had worked with the others for nearly seven months—with Huggie, who liked to be frightened; with George the arch scrounger; with Spuggy, who could sing the rarest songs; with Sadders, who is as brave as any man alive; with N'Soon, the dashing, of the tender skin; with Fat Boy, who loves "sustaining" food and dislikes frost; with Grimers and Cecil, best of artificers; with Potters and Orr and Moulders and the Flapper.

I cannot pay them a more sufficient tribute than the tribute of the Commander-in-Chief—

"Carrying despatches and messages at all hours of the day and night, in every kind of weather, and often traversing bad roads blocked with transport, they have been conspicuously successful in maintaining an extraordinary degree of efficiency in the service of communications.... No amount of difficulty or danger has ever checked the energy and ardour which has distinguished their corps throughout the operations."

LEONAUR

ALSO FROM LEONAUR

AVAILABLE IN SOFTCOVER OR HARDCOVER WITH DUST JACKET

DOING OUR 'BIT' *by Ian Hay*—Two Classic Accounts of the Men of Kitchener's 'New Army' During the Great War including *The First 100,000 & All In It.*

AN EYE IN THE STORM by *Arthur Ruhl*—An American War Correspondent's Experiences of the First World War from the Western Front to Gallipoli and Beyond.

STAND & FALL by *Joe Cassells*—A Soldier's Recollections of the 'Contemptible Little Army' and the Retreat from Mons to the Marne, 1914.

RIFLEMAN MACGILL'S WAR by *Patrick MacGill*—A Soldier of the London Irish During the Great War in Europe including *The Amateur Army, The Red Horizon & The Great Push.*

WITH THE GUNS *by C. A. Rose & Hugh Dalton*—Two First Hand Accounts of British Gunners at War in Europe During World War 1- Three Years in France with the Guns and With the British Guns in Italy.

EAGLES OVER THE TRENCHES *by James R. McConnell & William B. Perry*—Two First Hand Accounts of the American Escadrille at War in the Air During World War 1-Flying For France: With the American Escadrille at Verdun and Our Pilots in the Air.

THE BUSH WAR DOCTOR by *Robert V. Dolbey*—The Experiences of a British Army Doctor During the East African Campaign of the First World War.

THE 9TH—THE KING'S (LIVERPOOL REGIMENT) IN THE GREAT WAR 1914 - 1918 by *Enos H. G. Roberts*—Like many large cities, Liverpool raised a number of battalions in the Great War. Notable among them were the Pals, the Liverpool Irish and Scottish, but this book concerns the wartime history of the 9th Battalion – The Kings.

THE GAMBARDIER by *Mark Severn*—The experiences of a battery of Heavy artillery on the Western Front during the First World War.

FROM MESSINES TO THIRD YPRES by *Thomas Floyd*—A personal account of the First World War on the Western front by a 2/5th Lancashire Fusilier.

THE IRISH GUARDS IN THE GREAT WAR - VOLUME 1 by *Rudyard Kipling*—Edited and Compiled from Their Diaries and Papers Volume 1 The First Battalion.

THE IRISH GUARDS IN THE GREAT WAR - VOLUME 2 by *Rudyard Kipling*—Edited and Compiled from Their Diaries and Papers Volume 2 The Second Battalion.

LEONAUR

ALSO FROM LEONAUR

AVAILABLE IN SOFTCOVER OR HARDCOVER WITH DUST JACKET

CAPTAIN OF THE 95th (Rifles) *by Jonathan Leach*—An officer of Wellington's Sharpshooters during the Peninsular, South of France and Waterloo Campaigns of the Napoleonic Wars.

BUGLER AND OFFICER OF THE RIFLES *by William Green & Harry Smith* With the 95th (Rifles) during the Peninsular & Waterloo Campaigns of the Napoleonic Wars

BAYONETS, BUGLES AND BONNETS by *James 'Thomas' Todd*—Experiences of hard soldiering with the 71st Foot - the Highland Light Infantry - through many battles of the Napoleonic wars including the Peninsular & Waterloo Campaigns

THE ADVENTURES OF A LIGHT DRAGOON *by George Farmer & G.R. Gleig*—A cavalryman during the Peninsular & Waterloo Campaigns, in captivity & at the siege of Bhurtpore, India

THE COMPLEAT RIFLEMAN HARRIS *by Benjamin Harris as told to & transcribed by Captain Henry Curling*—The adventures of a soldier of the 95th (Rifles) during the Peninsular Campaign of the Napoleonic Wars

WITH WELLINGTON'S LIGHT CAVALRY *by William Tomkinson*—The Experiences of an officer of the 16th Light Dragoons in the Peninsular and Waterloo campaigns of the Napoleonic Wars.

SURTEES OF THE RIFLES by *William Surtees*—A Soldier of the 95th (Rifles) in the Peninsular campaign of the Napoleonic Wars.

ENSIGN BELL IN THE PENINSULAR WAR *by George Bell*—The Experiences of a young British Soldier of the 34th Regiment 'The Cumberland Gentlemen' in the Napoleonic wars.

WITH THE LIGHT DIVISION by *John H. Cooke*—The Experiences of an Officer of the 43rd Light Infantry in the Peninsula and South of France During the Napoleonic Wars

NAPOLEON'S IMPERIAL GUARD: FROM MARENGO TO WATERLOO by *J. T. Headley*—This is the story of Napoleon's Imperial Guard from the bearskin caps of the grenadiers to the flamboyance of their mounted chasseurs, their principal characters and the men who commanded them.

BATTLES & SIEGES OF THE PENINSULAR WAR by *W. H. Fitchett*—Corunna, Busaco, Albuera, Ciudad Rodrigo, Badajos, Salamanca, San Sebastian & Others

LEONAUR

ALSO FROM LEONAUR

AVAILABLE IN SOFTCOVER OR HARDCOVER WITH DUST JACKET

A JOURNAL OF THE SECOND SIKH WAR by *Daniel A. Sandford*—The Experiences of an Ensign of the 2nd Bengal European Regiment During the Campaign in the Punjab, India, 1848-49.

LAKE'S CAMPAIGNS IN INDIA by *Hugh Pearse*—The Second Anglo Maratha War, 1803-1807. Often neglected by historians and students alike, Lake's Indian campaign was fought against a resourceful and ruthless enemy-almost always superior in numbers to his own forces.

BRITAIN IN AFGHANISTAN 1: THE FIRST AFGHAN WAR 1839-42 by *Archibald Forbes*—Following over a century of the gradual assumption of sovereignty of the Indian Sub-Continent, the British Empire, in the form of the Honourable East India Company, supported by troops of the new Queen Victoria's army, found itself inevitably at the natural boundaries that surround Afghanistan. There it set in motion a series of disastrous events-the first of which was to march into the country at all.

BRITAIN IN AFGHANISTAN 2: THE SECOND AFGHAN WAR 1878-80 by *Archibald Forbes*—This the history of the Second Afghan War-another episode of British military history typified by savagery, massacre, siege and battles.

UP AMONG THE PANDIES by *Vivian Dering Majendie*—An outstanding account of the campaign for the fall of Lucknow. *This is a vital book of war as fought by the British Army of the mid-nineteenth century, but in truth it is also an essential book of war that will enthral military historians and general readers alike.*

BLOW THE BUGLE, DRAW THE SWORD by *W. H. G. Kingston*—The Wars, Campaigns, Regiments and Soldiers of the British & Indian Armies During the Victorian Era, 1839-1898.

INDIAN MUTINY 150th ANNIVERSARY: A LEONAUR ORIGINAL

MUTINY: 1857 by *James Humphries*—It is now 150 years since the 'Indian Mutiny' burst like an engulfing flame on the British soldiers, their families and the civilians of the Empire in North East India. The Bengal Native army arose in violent rebellion, and the once peaceful countryside became a battleground as Native sepoys and elements of the Indian population massacred their British masters and defeated them in open battle. As the tide turned, a vengeful army of British and loyal Indian troops repressed the insurgency with a savagery that knew no mercy. It was a time of fear and slaughter. James Humphries has drawn together the voices of those dreadful days for this commemorative book.

AVAILABLE ONLINE AT
www.leonaur.com
AND OTHER GOOD BOOK STORES

SC-1

LEONAUR

ALSO FROM LEONAUR

AVAILABLE IN SOFTCOVER OR HARDCOVER WITH DUST JACKET

ARMOURED CARS IN EDEN *by K. Roosevelt*—An American President's son serving in Rolls Royce armoured cars with the British in Mesopatamia & with the American Artillery in France during the First World War.

CHASSEUR OF 1914 by *Marcel Dupont*—Experiences of the twilight of the French Light Cavalry by a young officer during the early battles of the great war in Europe.

TROOP HORSE & TRENCH by *R.A. Lloyd*—The experiences of a British Lifeguardsman of the household cavalry fighting on the western front during the First World War 1914-18.

THE LONG PATROL by *George Berrie*—A Novel of Light Horsemen from Gallipoli to the Palestine campaign of the First World War.

THE EAST AFRICAN MOUNTED RIFLES *by C.J. Wilson*—Experiences of the campaign in the East African bush during the First World War

THE FIGHTING CAMELIERS *by Frank Reid*—The exploits of the Imperial Camel Corps in the desert and Palestine campaigns of the First World War.

WITH THE IMPERIAL CAMEL CORPS IN THE GREAT WAR by *Geoffrey Inchbald*—The story of a serving officer with the British 2nd battalion against the Senussi and during the Palestine campaign.

STEEL CHARIOTS IN THE DESERT by *S.C.Rolls*—The first world war experiences of a Rolls Royce armoured car driver with the Duke of Westminster in Libya and in Arabia with T.E. Lawrence.

CPSIA information can be obtained
at www.ICGtesting.com
Printed in the USA
LVHW111543041119
636284LV00013B/978/P

9 781846 773846